LOST
CORNWALL
*

This book is dedicated to my mother, Valerie Randles.

First published in 2007 by
Birlinn Limited
West Newington House
10 Newington Road
Edinburgh
EH9 1QS

www.birlinn.co.uk

Hbk
ISBN13: 978 1 84158 604 5
ISBN10: 1 84158 604 8

Pbk
ISBN13: 978 1 84158 649 6
ISBN10: 1 84158 649 8

British Library Cataloguing-in-Publication Data
A catalogue record for this book is available
from the British Library.

Editor Alison Moss
Design Andrew Sutterby

Printed and bound in China by 1010, China

LOST
CORNWALL

Joanna Thomas

BIRLINN

CONTENTS

ACKNOWLEDGEMENTS

I would like to acknowledge the great help of Peter Andrews, postcard dealer from West Country Cards (tel: 07866 554 216) who spent many patient hours helping me source suitable images.

Thanks also to all the staff at Cornwall Centre (Cornish Studies Library) in Redruth; The National Maritime Museum, Falmouth; Cornwall Record Office, Truro; Royal Institution Of Cornwall at Royal Cornwall Museum; Isles of Scilly Museum, St Mary's; Penlee House and Museum, Penzance; The Cornish Methodist Historical Association in particular the Rev. Colin Short for his time and patience; Sylvia Smith with her historical collection of Mawnan Smith.

One of the many ancient granite Cornish 'hedges' in Penwith built of stone and filled with earth.

To Stephen Thomas for his invaluable help taking all the photographs of Cornwall as it is in the present day.

I especially want to mention Jim Hall, Head of Journalism Studies at University College Falmouth for his support and encouragement over the years.

PICTURE CREDITS

Courtesy of Peter Andrews, West Country Cards front cover and pp. 7, 13, 14, 21, 24, 25, 34, 35, 37, 47, 53, 61, 71, 72, 74, 77, 81, 83, 85, 86, 88, 90, 91, 114, 115, 116, 117, 118, 119, 120, 125, 129, 130, 132, 133, 134, 136, 138, 140, 141, 145, 146, 147, 148, 150, 151, 155, 156, 157, 158, 159, 160, 166; Stephen Thomas back cover and pp. 49, 51, 63, 64, 113, 127, 142, 162, 168, 170, 171, 172, 173; Penlee House Gallery and Museum, Penzance pp. 93, 97, 100, 109, 112; H.N. Shore (later known as Lord Teignmouth) illustrations from The Cornish Magazine circa 1899 pp. 169, 180, 182; The Methodist Church UK p. 6; Cornwall Centre/Kresenn Kernow (Cornish Studies Library) pp. 16, 22, 26, 27, 28, 44, 45, 52, 143, 154.

INTRODUCTION

To visit Cornwall is to visit a land set apart. The Cornish consider it a country in its own right and refer to neighbouring Devon as 'up country' in England. For those born on Cornish soil there is identification with a land separated by the sea and River Tamar; they are a people set apart. Those who consider themselves to have a birthright connection with their native Kernow (its Celtic name) identify with a movement that to some extent celebrates concepts of 'Cornish distinctiveness'. Many see themselves as a separate race and enthusiastically assert their sense of difference.

There are those who strive to rekindle the use of the Cornish language and are zealous in their endeavours to restore and maintain old customs, feast-day ceremonies and a sense of unique cultural heritage. There are varying interpretations of the reasoning behind this movement. For some it is almost a religion, for others a way of identifying with their family's history; there are political overtones voiced by some sectors, while others are taken up with Celtic origins and see it as a profound form of ethnic expression. Representations of this movement are sometimes symbolised by flying the Cornish flag, wearing Cornish tartan and marking out ancient ceremonies. These 'emblems' function as signs that exemplify concepts, ideas and feelings connected to Cornish identity and heritage.

There is still an emphatic element in the Duchy that continues to be persistent in the cause of Kernow, especially now Great Britain is forging links with the wider European community in the 2000s. More than ever the Cornish are eager to redress certain aspects of history that have amalgamated them with the rest of Britain without distinction or recognition as a unique people.

Cornish culture is perhaps a difficult concept to define. More traditional definitions of the term embody the best that has been thought and said in a society, such as Cornish music, poetry and artistic achievement, and it is perhaps partly useful to see some of Cornish culture in this way.

In a social science context the term 'culture' has been used to refer to the distinctive way of life of a people, community or social group, so it can be used to describe the shared values of a group or society. Thus Cornish culture depends on participants meaningfully interpreting what is happening in the region around them, and making sense of the place in broadly similar ways, by sharing meanings, for example, through feast-day celebrations, such as Lafrowda Festival, or Helston Flora Day, or Cornish Rugby. These activities give the collective a sense of shared values that underpin a group identity.

Unfortunately, the concept of being Cornish does not have any one fixed, unchanging meaning, but is part of a growing consensus that, over time, has been stated by some and seen as contentious by others. Despite this lack of absolute continuity and the fragmentation of some cultural definitions there is nevertheless a sense of shared roots and a common history among the native Cornish, even though the distinguishing cultural markers are less easy to define.

Lost Cornwall delves into aspects of the past that, together, have shaped this common history, uncovering features that are perhaps somewhat hidden to the general populous. Its aim is to recognise in writing what is perhaps not straightaway recognisable in a place, from a simple cursory glance.

Whatever the motivations and belief systems of certain sections of the population in Cornwall and the controversies and contentions raised from their stance, there can be no denying that they are expressing a deep affinity to place; a place that has held a fascination for so many different groups, a prevalent unifying identification with the land of Cornwall. Artists, writers, geologists, archeologists and ecologists, to name but a few, have all staked a claim to association with Cornish soil in some measure.

Cornwall has the capacity to capture hearts with mystical qualities, sometimes beyond reason. For those who have been adopted by Cornwall there is also an indelible affinity to a place that has accommodated so many migrant settlers. The wildness of the moors and cliffs somehow seem to empathise with the lost and isolated, with those who are devoid of their own cultural roots. They have found a landscape that epitomises their own life experiences, offering them solace in some way. For them Cornwall is a sanctuary, a safe harbour for their soul.

This is not a book written by an expert but rather by somebody who is in love with Cornwall. This is not a rational or reasoned emotional identification, but rather, an instinctive affinity to a landscape. To be away from Cornwall is to be bereft, to live away from the sea is to experience loss. In many ways this book is an introduction, a taster that will hopefully kindle an interest and a desire to delve deeper.

In writing this book one is only too aware of the range of published material, of the other researchers and writers who have given their life's work to a specific area of expertise. There are those fascinated with all things nautical, or individuals who have studied the workings of a steam locomotive and its history, for decades. This book hopes to honour the work of these experts by deciphering some of their findings for the reader. It is hoped that the book might break down some of the in-depth academic researches into a more palatable form, enabling greater accessibility to Cornwall's rich history.

Many consider Cornwall to be a place to spend a summer holiday – idyllic stretches of golden sand and exuberant surf beckon the crowds south-west of the Tamar bridge. There are those who long to immerse themselves in the atmosphere of the moorlands, to amble through apparently wild, uncharted territory, escaping from daily pressures. These visitors' demands enliven Cornwall's economy, forcing its inhabitants to look beyond the penin-sula and forge connections with the world beyond. Among the seasonal influx are those who come year after year, unable to shake off Cornwall's allure. They, too, have gained a sense of identification, based on a sense of place. It is often said that so far south, life is taken at a slower pace, that the lifestyle is more relaxed, or that in some ways Cornwall is not as wrapped up in the modern world.

These statements, if true, may be more significant still to those intrigued by the past. Cornwall has retained something of the ancient. Even though, by necessity, modernity has impinged upon most aspects of Cornish life, the past has been remarkably preserved. A general lack of development has meant that previous ventures, such as mining or smelting, have merely been laid down to rest rather than cleared or superseded by new initiatives. As certain industries went into decline, they left their imprint, and in many cases the buildings and landmarks have remained in ruins, nature rather than man's fresh enterprise obscuring their former significance.

It is hoped that *Lost Cornwall* will stimulate the reader's sense of intrigue, precipitating further exploration of places influenced by the past. In many ways this is something to celebrate. Cornwall has managed to hold on to its precious heritage – the mine buildings, fishermen's cottages, old farm-steads – and although this book is concerned with that which is now lost, in some instances it considers that which has also been retained.

Every town and village has marks to uncover, indicators or distinguish-ing features linked to some previous use. As a book, the contents will no doubt raise many more questions than it will answer, but in a humble way it is intended to create interest across the generations. Together, families can endeavour to find out more of what has been lost to us by visiting one of the local museums, historic landmarks or heritage trails that hold far more information than can be offered in these pages. The past still clings to what is left behind and therein lies the intrigue.

CHAPTER 1

METHODISM

Behind the granite façades, high windows and sturdy doors of many Methodist chapels throughout the Duchy, there are forums rather like a stage, in which the tales of lives have been outworked. As we pass the historic architecture we can easily lose sight of the humanity beyond the iron railings and crafted stone masonry.

The births, marriages and deaths of generations of worshippers have been proclaimed, and their convictions affirmed, before a community of believers. With the rites of ceremony, however simple, they upheld marriage and baptism and a belief in life everlasting beyond the grave. Yet the enormity of each chapel's role in the community has changed, and in some cases has been lost for good, as doors have closed and there has been a change of use.

Nearly every Cornish town or village has a chapel or two, each bearing the signs of years of faithful service and stirrings of spirituality within. These Methodist buildings are commonplace, yet their profound loss of significance is easily hidden amongst the colourful signs of our time, commercial buildings or busy roads that usurp their consequence. Now the high-street shops and businesses crowd out chapel buildings that were once the centre of many townsfolk's lives. It is perhaps hard to fully envisage, in our predominantly secular society, how crucial the role of the Church was in our not-too-distant past.

The extent to which whole communities embraced the Christian message, through the preaching of John Wesley and his fellow ministers, is well documented in his diaries. Uneducated miners, fishermen, rural workers and their families were converted to Methodism in their droves from the late 1700s, and to some extent shunned the conventions of the established churches.

Methodism was Cornwall's principal religious denomination in 1851 and the Duchy had the highest proportion of chapels nationally at that time. The mining communities in South Wales were similarly affected by Methodism, but there was still no national equal to the number of dissenting places of worship in England and Wales than in Cornwall.

This non-conformist movement, parochially dubbed as 'Wezleans', met initially in homes throughout the Duchy, yet as numbers in these societies increased, it became necessary to build chapels to accommodate the crowds. Initially these were simple in architectural design, in some cases not dissimilar to agricultural buildings, yet as the aspirations and prosperity of Methodism grew the designs developed into a distinct characteristic style.

A non-conformist chapel needed to be licensed by an Anglican bishop, archdeacon or the justices as a place of worship for dissenters. To begin with places were built as preaching houses for the Methodist's mid-week meetings and they were later called 'chapels' once worship took place on a Sunday.

Functionality was the main influence in the early days; they were intended to perform a purpose and were similar in design to Cornish farm barns. Rural cob stone and slate roofs were often all that was required. A perfect example of this is preserved at Gwithian near St Ives Bay, built in 1810; it is the last thatched Methodist chapel in the region.

The floors of these original preaching houses would be of beaten earth, and worshippers were expected to wrap up warm, as there was often no form of heating. High-backed pews, arranged in rows, were crafted with the specific purpose of keeping draughts away from the backs of necks.

There was, however, a sense of seemliness in the neat layout and decorum in the way things were arranged inside, similar to domestic arrangements at that time. These were community houses that derived architectural conventions from the Cornish countryside, rather than from classical and religious architectural traditions.

Over time, the more prosperous members of Cornish society chose to affiliate with Chapel rather than Church. Wealthy traders, merchants and mining agents took to attending Society meetings on a Sunday. This in turn changed the character of the rough and ready meetings and created a more respectable element to proceedings. Industrial and municipal architectural design influenced chapel building in the Victorian era and internally the chapels followed a prescribed form.

Great cavernous chapels were built with the injection of income, some with the capacity to seat 1,000 and often with revival numbers in mind. The Methodists had a hope for 'bountiful harvests of souls' as they planned, preached and prayed for their community's conversion. Such visionary earnestness was most probably influenced by the population growth of that era, as Cornwall doubled its population between 1801 and 1861, perhaps giving church planners a sense of inflated optimism. Certainly, pockets of revival justified such enthusiasm but other influences were to bear upon chapel attendance.

Since the peak of the late 1850s there has been a general decline in Methodist membership. This is no doubt inextricably linked to economic conditions in the region and specifically the large-scale emigration between 1861 and 1921. Copper and tin mining was adversely affected due to the market depression in the 1840s and 1850s, and with the development of the railways those in the carrying trade found themselves without employment.

In many respects the decline in chapel or church attendance today is reflective of a sociological change, taking place nationally, although worldwide there continues to be an increase in Methodist membership. In 2003, the 300th year of John Wesley's birth, the membership in Britain was about 314,000 and decreasing by 2 per cent a year.

What makes Cornwall's fall in religious observance unique is that Methodism had such a profound impact on Cornish life in the past. It is hard to imagine revivals taking place in the same way today and the distinctive style of Wesley's preaching will never quite be matched again. Communities of worshippers still practise their faith according to Methodist traditions, many with several generations of Methodists in their family history, but more often there are struggling congregations with the burden of preserving Grade II listed buildings, the legacies from a more pious past.

Travel along any of the main roads through Cornwall and sooner or later you will come across one of the many wayside chapel buildings; they stand resiliently it seems. Others are hidden in isolated districts, with few signs of human habitation nearby to warrant such a prominent position in the Cornish landscape. Rather than nucleated villages these chapels were erected for scattered hamlets and farmsteads. Temple Chapel, close to the A30 near Bodmin Moor, typifies the rural chapel in an isolated hamlet. There are other wayside chapels at New Mill near Gulval (now a house) and Rinsey close to Mounts Bay (closed in 1950) and at Roseworthy, between Camborne and Hayle, which has now been restored from ruins by its new residential occupants. All are similarly situated away from main thoroughfares.

Before the myriad of A roads that network the Cornish countryside, there would once have been only rough tracks that led to remote farms. The workers would rarely venture out except for market and chapel, and so to the motorist today the full significance of such journeys is perhaps lost. Whole farming communities would have gathered together for Sunday worship or mid-week prayer, with neighbouring farmers making the journey in all weathers on horseback or foot. They'd gain a rare glimpse of life beyond their boundary hedges, a chance to relate to those outside their immediate community.

It is perhaps the social element that we tend to disregard when we look up at the external representation of a Methodist chapel, the stones are but a poor portrayal of the deep human yearnings that must have taken place in these intimate times.

There were 'Love feasts' where tea, plain biscuits or bread, and water were shared. Hymns would be sung, prayers offered and members encouraged to speak about spiritual experiences in these small informal gatherings.

Fellow believers shared their needs for prayer, maybe sickness or family problems, each a tale of human struggle met with compassion from others, who were willing to carry some of the burden. There would have been a deep need for repentance as individuals sought to live holier lives and to leave their sins behind.

Part of the success of this emerging denomination was the way in which it was organised. Groups of twelve members, called Societies, met every week for instruction and prayer. Examination of one's conscience was encouraged while preparing to take communion in the parish church the following Sunday, and mutual admonishment was carried out in Society meetings, all with the aim of creating a more fruitful and puritanical Christian path. It was a time when the leader of the group could support and oversee any difficulties any of the believers might have. This unique meeting meant that new converts and those struggling with their faith could be encouraged, rather than left in isolation to the next service in the church.

Certainly this social side to the Methodist Church would have made Society gatherings enjoyable for any who were remotely interested in the affairs of their neighbours. A sense of belonging would be valued and a genuine belief in celebrating life, in all its stages, would be accomplished through the different styles of meeting.

But to appreciate why so many chapels were built in rural communities it is necessary to explore the full impact of Methodism in the Duchy from the late-eighteenth century to the mid-nineteenth century and consider how the religious character of the region was transformed at this time.

In a public census taken throughout England and Wales on 30 March 1851 church attendances were counted. Of the 356,000 population of Cornwall, 49 per cent were to be found in church that Sunday.

Obviously the cynical mind can imagine all the spurious means used to cajole the less than eager worshipper. However, of these 174,000 'faithful', the clear majority, 65 per cent, attended Methodist worship. Church of England parishioners accounted for a smaller 27 per cent, the remainder being a few hundred Roman Catholics, 10,000 Congregationalists and Baptists and few hundred other non-conformists. Despite there being a disparity between Methodist membership figures and attendance figures on that Sunday, what the census provides us with is a clear indication of what a stronghold the denomination had in the land south of the River Tamar.

Cornwall's response to Methodism is by no means reflective of the rest of the British Isles but its popularity could have something to do with the rapid growth of population between 1801 and 1861 and the expansion of mining into areas where the Church of England was structurally weak.

It is perhaps Cornwall's isolation that made it seem a less than comfortable and inviting prospect for the established Church of England's clergy. Many of the rural parishes and dioceses were large and straggling, making pastoral visits unmanageable and prey to problems of poor communication. Ecclesiastical provision was sporadic and church services were held irregularly as a consequence. Methodism, by contrast, reached rural areas, scattered mining settlements and coastal villages in a way that the established Church failed to do, perhaps because it relied on a team of lay men and women rather than just one clergyman.

There is no doubt that the rise in numbers is intrinsically linked to the population growth in general, as the tin mines and quarries offered employment throughout the peninsula. However, there is also an extraordinary tale of endeavour as one particular clergyman, John Wesley, resiliently faced opposition and violence, bore the rigours of travelling in a land with few roads, on foot and horseback, to bring his old-time message to the Cornish people.

It took place in a way that has not be seen or responded to in the same way before or since and the places of worship stand as reminders of a cultural phenomenon.

The Pioneer Preacher

To fully understand how Methodism made its mark on Cornish culture it is perhaps worth briefly considering its founder member and his motivations. As a son of an Anglican clergyman, educated at Oxford, John Wesley sought to honour God in all aspects of his daily life. His mother, Susanna, had a great influence over him, in as much as she had brought him up diligently to follow prescribed routines. She had such a large brood of children that it was perhaps necessary for her to instill such values in them for the household to maintain some sense of order. However, she was also devout in her religion and longed to see her offspring, including John and his

John Wesley as a young man circa 1730s.

brother Charles, keep to the Christian faith.

John continued to be self-disciplined in his early adult life at university, ever mindful of his Christian upbringing. He rose early for prayer, regularly fasted and routinely set aside times for Bible study along with other similarly devout young men at Oxford, including his brother Charles. It was this methodology in daily living that gained these earnest undergraduates the derogatory name of 'Methodists', along with other nicknames such as 'The Holy Club'. Their routine activities were to become part of Methodism's distinctive precepts and were to inspire Cornish Methodist's weekly schedules for generations.

Despite setting aside time for devotions in non-religious venues, Wesley was earnest in his allegiance to the Church of England and he considered the taking of communion to be paramount in a Christian believer's life. Initially he only ever intended to seek the deepening of his spiritual life and he longed to bring a vibrant spirituality to the Anglican Church. However, those he converted had different views, and certainly in Cornwall Methodism became distinct as its membership grew.

Going on to study a Masters degree, Wesley was to become a deacon in the Anglican Church. It was fully anticipated by his parents that he would

St Mary's Wesleyan Chapel, Truro, in 1932. This style of chapel typifies the larger Methodist chapel and was built in 1830. The internal design reflects the beliefs of the chapel founders. There is no altar, as in the traditional Anglican churches, as a non-conformist would consider one unnecessary. They would hold to a view that an altar was associated with Old Testament practices of priesthood, or perhaps had Pagan connotations. Instead, the pulpit is given the main position, so that that everyone can see and hear the preacher clearly. A simple table and sometimes a communion rail is often all that is used to administer bread and wine. The organ with balcony choir stalls is also central to the design of the chapel, primarily because hymn singing is such an integral part of collective worship.

continue in his father's footsteps and perhaps take over his parish in Lincolnshire. But other influences were to bear on Wesley's ministry, including a trip overseas to Georgia where, en route, he came in contact with a group of Moravians. This community of Protestant believers from Germany so impressed Wesley on board ship, with their calm demeanour in the throes of a near-fatal storm, that he was profoundly moved to question his own depth of faith in relation to theirs.

It wasn't until three years later, when he had returned to London, that he was to have what he considered to be a genuine conversion, on 24 May 1738. This was a deeper spiritual experience such as he considered the Moravians to feel. It was the turning point in his life when he testified to being 'saved'.

Such was Wesley's desire to see men and women's lives changed in the way that his had been, by what he describes as a touch of God in his heart, that he surrendered his life to the cause. Wesley longed to outwork the relevance of his beliefs practically and he had the full support of Charles and a dear friend, George Whitefield, in his evangelistic zeal.

Even though the established churches were to reject him and bar him from preaching in their pulpits, Wesley was encouraged by Whitefield and began to preach in the open air to anyone who would listen. Thousands did.

Church in the Hedgerows

Church leaders today are faced with the issue of dwindling numbers in their congregations. Inter-denominational conferences often raise the issue of how to make church services relevant to a society where the majority has turned its back on the Christian faith. There are debates as to why Wesley's preaching was so successful. It must surely be partly due to fact that he met the people where they were going about their business – out in the streets and rural byways – rather than expecting them to enter into a church building to hear his message. Perhaps it was this element to his ministry that made his preaching so accessible to the 'common man'.

It seems that Wesley was moved by compassion by what he considered to be the plight of ordinary humanity. He worked in an era when there was no state provision for the unemployed, sick or destitute. Living conditions in population centres were renowned for being without sanitation, and disease and premature death was rife.

He was familiar with the social difficulties in the city – gin houses, prostitution and the surge in abandoned or orphaned children. So committed was he to see change that he was prepared to give up the comforts of a gentleman and live part of his ministry almost as a vagrant. He disciplined himself to live a life of simplicity in order to set aside a significant amount of his income to give to the poor. These financial considerations were to be part of Methodist culture in the future and provision would be made for orphans, widows and other needy sectors of society, to prevent the necessity of them entering the dreaded workhouses.

Yet it was the spiritual needs of the working classes that Wesley considered to be of paramount importance. He was so driven by a desire to see change from within a man or woman's heart, that he was to face extreme opposition, violent persecution and even betrayal from those closest to him.

He had such an energy and a passion that many others would no doubt have said he was verging on the insane or at best close to religious mania. People who hold his memory dear are admiring of his single-mindedness and dedication. Whatever your view of this preacher man, it is undeniable that his commitment to the cause meant that Cornish culture and indeed that of the British Isles was changed irreversibly. At the time of his death in 1791 he is thought to have preached 40,000 sermons, given away more than £30,000 and was founder of a denomination that is recognised and respected worldwide.

Cornwall

In 1743 Wesley crossed the River Tamar for the first time, fully intent on persuading every Cornishman of his need for salvation. At the time of Wesley's first visit, there were already over 100 Methodists gathering regularly at St Ives and it was here that he decided to head first. Using St Ives as his initial preaching venue, he then travelled throughout west Cornwall and even ventured to the Isles of Scilly in a borrowed boat.

Despite the frequently arduous travelling conditions in extreme weather, he endeavoured to preach the gospel up to five times in a day throughout Cornwall. He was to visit almost annually (more than thirty times) over a period of forty-five years.

Wesley would have looked a slightly eccentric clergyman, reading scriptures and sermon notes on horseback, or nose down to the pages of a book as he trekked on foot through the Cornish moors. He preferred to 'wear' his own hair, rather than a fashionable wig, to save money for the poor, and although his quality clothing was 'gentlemanly', it was by no means ostentatious. So it was perhaps his preaching style that was so arresting rather than a grand appearance.

He held a deep conviction in what he considered to be humans' damned state and offered a carefully considered rescue plan through the gospel. He won over a generation with his magnetism and, unlike the established Church, he made no distinctions between gentry and pauper. His message was for everyone.

Opponents and Riots

In those early years the opposition to Methodist preaching was widespread throughout the Duchy and the rest of the British Isles. The Anglican clergy, supported by those with social standing, were openly hostile and encouraged their congregations to behave likewise. The clerics and landowning dignitaries encouraged angry mobs, often induced by alcohol, to drive Wesley and his followers away using physical force.

One could easily assume, because of the uproar he caused in many towns, that he was a dramatic 'thunderous' preacher, yet by all accounts his demeanour and style were unassuming. There is no denying his mode of address was both forthright and challenging, which may have led to criticisms that he was too provocative. He wasn't afraid to speak of the terrors of hell, yet he presented his sermons in a disciplined and plain manner. He would pen them and reuse them as appropriate and copies of them can be read today.

During the 1740s Wesley faced ferocious opposition and hardships at the hands of persecuting crowds. Certainly Wesley's revolutionary approach to preaching out of doors, incited incredible responses, not all of them positive.

To illustrate how incompatible his ways were with his clergy contemporaries, it is insightful to read his journal on 11 August 1753. 'The rain stopped at twelve, and gave me an opportunity of preaching in the market place at Camelford. I saw only one person in the congregation who was not deeply serious. That one (which I was sorry to hear) was the Curate of the parish.'

The main difficulty the Church of England had was that Wesley was a member of the clergy who paid little regard to parish boundaries by preaching on other clergymen's patches. Had he been a dissenter, such as a Baptist or Quaker, they could have dealt with him as such; however, he raised hostility among his fellow Anglicans because he failed to defer to Church protocol.

Despite several early Methodist preachers being violently set upon, and sometimes injured, most of the preaching engagements were eventually safeguarded by individual magistrates: they evidently saw persecution and intervened. Before the Toleration Act of 1689 all non-conformist congregations were repressed and persecuted by the authorities. Since the Act, the restrictive measures lessened and non-conformists gained a measure of tolerance and legal recognition and protection. Yet despite this protection the opposition to Wesley and his fellow workers continued sporadically throughout his ministry.

On Wednesday, 8 August 1753, he wrote in his journal and depicted tensions that often arose when he presented himself to a crowd:

We were invited to Mevagissey, a small town on the south sea. As soon as we entered the town, many ran together, crying, 'See, the Methodees are come.' But they only gaped and stared; so that we returned unmolested to the house I was to preach at, a mile from the town. Many serious people were waiting for us, but most of them deeply ignorant. While I was showing them the first principles of Christianity, many of the rabble from the town came up.

They looked as fierce as lions; but in a few minutes changed their countenance, and stood still. Toward the close, some began to laugh and talk, who grew more boisterous after I had concluded. But I walked straight through the midst of them, and took horse without any interruption.

Wesley had the ability to win over the fractious masses and there are vivid descriptions of violent threats at various times through his ministry. This includes a famous riot that took place at Falmouth in the summer of 1745, when a mob threatened his life.

A horde surrounded the house where Wesley was staying. At this time Falmouth was the most cosmopolitan port in the British Isles. Far from being a quaint Cornish coastal town, it was a major commercial and military centre with small packet vessels dispatching Royal Mail, bullion and government officials around the globe. It was to this international trading port that Wesley sought to bring the Gospel.

Although it is not clear from his diaries who was in the rioting crowd, what is mentioned is that his hosts fled their own home leaving Wesley to face the danger alone. One can imagine a rough and unruly mob, some hardened sailors perhaps, or drunks making murderous threats.

Wesley's account describes how he remained steadfast within the house until the door was finally broken down. But rather than run away and hide, he stood up and went out to face his adversaries. He addressed the whole gathering, purposely removing his hat so that everyone could see his face, and then went into the middle of the street. From here he challenged the crowd asking them if he had wronged them in some way, using gentle reason to subdue the noise. They allowed him to speak and he eventually left the scene unscathed. One is left wondering what it was about him that enabled him to deal with such situations so peaceably. He writes that he considered his deliverance in Falmouth to be the working of 'the hand of God'.

Ten years later he writes in his journal on 2 September:

We went to Falmouth. The town is not now what it was ten years since: all is quiet from one end to the other. I had thoughts of preaching on the hill near the church; but the violent wind made it impracticable: so I was obliged to stay in our own room. The people could hear in the yard likewise, and the adjoining houses; and all were deeply attentive.

A Travel Journal

In his personal diaries he gives accounts of his times in Cornwall; some days are just a paragraph long while others offer greater insight into his travels. On initial reading one is instantly struck by the number of miles he covers each day. The stamina needed to endure such distances would tax most people, even by modern modes of transport. Yet it barely seems possible that he could so easily move from town to town on horseback without much time for recuperation.

For instance, on 30 July 1755 he was in Truro and later in the day 12 miles away at Redruth, where he preached on an empty stomach, he recalls, as no one there thought to give him food or drink. The next day, a Sunday, he travelled a few miles to Gwennap, where he preached to several thousand but found none of them attentive! He travelled 7 miles by 1 July to Penryn, then on to Falmouth by the following afternoon and towards Helston, a distance of 12 miles, later that day. Despite heavy rain he travelled 18 miles to Newlyn, for a day of preaching in the streets, before being in St Just, a further 7 miles, by the Saturday.

Each of Wesley's daily updates include accounts of preaching engagements, some starting as early as 5 a.m., and up to as many as five a day. There are accounts of impromptu meetings with notable characters, times of confrontation and notes of genuine pastoral consideration for those he came across. From these spontaneous movements, from town to town, with chance meetings with ordinary people, an organised body developed, spread and established itself.

Wesley frequently spoke to small crowds in the street or on his travels from rural homestead to homestead, finding accommodation where it was offered and relying on Cornish folks' goodwill for sustenance. The most famous of his resting houses is Trewint at Five Lanes on Bodmin Moor (now close to the A30). In 1743, Elizabeth Isbell, the wife of a journeyman stonemason, Digory, gave refreshments to two of Wesley's fellow workers as they came to make advance preparations for Wesley's first visit. John Nelson and John Downes were travelling on the isolated route from Launceston when Elizabeth offered them hospitality in her home. This would be the first of many visits for Methodist preachers and she was instantly struck by how the visiting men knelt to pray spontaneously 'without a book'. Digory was moved to establish a Methodist Society in his home as time went on, which flourished.

However, the cottage became a redundant meeting place once chapels were built. It fell into ruin, and may have been lost for good, but fortunately it was restored in 1950. It is now open to the public and is thought to be the smallest Methodist preaching place in the world. It has a distinct rudimentary style, with white-washed cob walls and scrubbed flagstone floor, acting as a reminder of an era of pioneering preaching that was as unique as it was fervent. This lowly home would be as influential in establishing the Christian faith as any of the great churches, or even Truro's cathedral, in Cornwall's history. It was the very first place Wesley stayed and saw him and his fellow preachers return on numerous occasions.

As time went on countless Cornish folk offered preachers respite and food. Along the coastal road from St Ives to St Just is the former home of John and Alice Daniel at Rosemergy, where Wesley and his preachers stayed year after year.

In the formative years, groups or 'Societies' built up almost entirely from preaching in the open air and meeting in private homes. Open-air preaching, once chapels were built, became a thing of the past. There were a number of meadows around St Ives and Mullion where Wesley is said to have preached, as well as public places in towns such as Falmouth, St Austell and Redruth where there was a natural vantage point.

Falmouth's Central Methodist Church (1961) dominates 'The Moor' in the town centre with its imposing proportions. It stands today as a representation of how prominent Methodism was when it was reconstructed in 1956 after being damaged in the war. Inside there are portraits of John and Charles Wesley, along with significant objects of remembrance that highlight the ministries of preachers in the past.

ABOVE: The village of Lanner's Wesleyan Chapel and Schools (1904) stands high on the hill and can be seen from across the valley towards the intensive tin mining region of Pool and Redruth. BELOW: This photograph, taken in 1924, demonstrates the prominence of its location in the landscape around Lanner and Carnmarth.

Although Wesley could legally preach in an Anglican pulpit his revolutionary ways meant that he was shunned and excluded from many parishes. This was no doubt a painful rebuff for Wesley who considered himself to be a communicant of the Church of England even on his deathbed. When considering the theology that was upheld and taught within the Methodist Societies, there is little to quibble over as all the fundamental doctrines concur with mainstream Protestant beliefs. Wesley and his like-minded friends were, however, rejected and barred from many Anglican pulpits for decades.

Understandably, he was seen as a threat to the established Church and although he wasn't strictly a dissenter, because he still upheld Anglican beliefs and practices, he was nonetheless creating a stir among the ecclesiastical hierarchy and was dubbed 'subversive'.

Wesley had expected that converts would become more devout and attend their local parish church after responding to Methodist preaching. However, many found the weekday meetings more relevant in the 'house churches' or 'preaching houses'.

One venue that still remains and is used by Methodists today is Gwennap Pit. It is considered by some to be a hollow that has resulted from mining subsidence, although this has never be confirmed. Wesley made no secret of the fact that it was his favourite open-air preaching location in Cornwall and is by far the most famous. This amphitheatre, located on the outskirts of Redruth, is in a rural scenic setting. As a preacher known to engage vast crowds, even Wesley must have been surprised to find himself before an estimated assembly of 32,000 people on one occasion.

If one considers how Wesley was personally rejected and persecuted by other Christians and then went on to be threatened by fierce crowds, it is a wonder that he persisted in his lifelong mission. Even his wife began a campaign against him, deliberately slandering his name and bringing his integrity into question; yet despite these and many other difficulties he continued to preach regularly.

He gives a vivid account of a time of sickness after preaching in Newlyn in July 1753. He was taken ill with diarrhoea, which he demurely called a 'looseness', for several days. Yet he carries on, regardless of the vomiting, cramps and headaches, preaching at Ludgvan, a village outside Penzance, then on to Helston, a journey of 15 miles. He seems to be able to endure this punishing ordeal by drinking claret and water.

In his journal, dated 1 August 1753, he writes:

> At half an hour after two in the morning, my disorder came with more violence than ever. The cramp likewise returned; sometimes in my feet or hand, sometimes in my thighs, my side, or my throat. I had also a continual sickness, and a sensation of fulness [sic] at my

This photograph, taken circa 1907, depicts the enormity of a preaching engagement at Gwennap Pit. It evokes a sense of what it must have been like in Wesley's time and typifies Methodist culture during the 1940s and '50s. Women with their hats and men dressed in their best suits create a sense of decency through their demeanour.

stomach, as if it were ready to burst. I took a vomit; but it hardly wrought at all: nor did anything I took make any alteration. Thus I continued all day, and all the following night; yet this I could not particularly observe – I had no headache, no colic, nor any pain, (only the cramp) from first to last.

It was from a house in Camborne, four days into this bout of sickness, that he called for a doctor from Redruth, who prescribed some rhubarb, which he vomited up again. One can only imagine how his hosts would have considered this man with such an extraordinary reputation, as he lost all dignity, reduced to a vomiting wretch unable to leave his bed. Yet remarkably he preached three days later and continued on his travels as soon as he was able.

This illustrates what a driven and earnest man he must have been.

Intense and obsessed by his vision and calling, he was prepared to endure almost anything to share the Christian faith. This passion must have been infectious and no doubt his laymen would have relied on his instructions and been inspired by his fervour and enthusiasm.

On reflection one wonders whether it was the pain of rejection that goaded him forward at times or perhaps a belligerence in the face of so much opposition. After all, he had lost everything he held dear; the love and companionship of his wife, the respect of many Bishops and clergymen, as well as acceptance within many sectors of respectable society. He was outcast, ridiculed and as such of 'no reputation'. Essentially he had nothing to lose by following his course of action. Perhaps this painful process meant he could identify more fully with those who were socially marginalised, individuals who found themselves outside the established Church because they were uneducated, poorly dressed, uncouth and unable to enter into civilised Church culture. Methodism gave women (legally unequal to men), reformed drunkards, the uneducated and the ill-bred a chance of redemption. Wesley believed in a God of new beginnings and as such strove with every sinew in his body and with every sigh of prayer to bring hope to a generation.

A People's Man
Wesley gained acceptance as he persisted. By the summer of 1747 he was able to note how he was received peaceably in almost every place and considered it to be a strange change of circumstances. On 30 July he writes that there is not a single 'Huzza' in St Ives and marvels at the civility of the world at that time. Momentarily, the jeering opponents had allowed him to carry on with his preaching unhindered.

He uses an interesting choice of words because Huzza means to 'cheer'. This may mean that crowds had gathered to cheer or mock previously, although it is unclear why he chose to use a word that is usually associated with a jubilant greeting. Maybe he was relieved to be an accepted part of the community at last, able to travel around without causing too much of a stir.

However, it was not always so agreeable. Later on, by early autumn 1748, Wesley found himself dealing with a less favourable crowd in Newlyn. An extract from his journal on 25 September demonstrates how, despite the rabble's initial hostility, he apparently subdues the crowds with his words:

> I reached Newlyn a little after four. Here was a congregation of quite a different sort – a rude, gaping, starring rabble-rout; some or other of whom were throwing dirt or stones continually. But before

I was done, all were quiet and still; and some looked as if they felt what was spoken. We came to St Ives about seven: the room would nothing near contain the congregation; but they stood in the orchard all round, and could hear perfectly well.

This capacity to influence groups of people is demonstrated in St Ives on Wednesday, 25 July 1753. He meets with the Methodist Society, so he reports, and all are confessed buyers or dealers in un-customed goods (easy pickings for a seafaring community). So grave is this 'abomination' to Wesley that he sets aside a day to meet with the members concerned. He plainly rebukes them and threatens to have nothing more to do with them if they don't give up buying and selling in this way. Of course they earnestly promise to renounce their black-market trading, but it is interesting that it takes them until Friday to do so and Wesley gives no insight into Thursday's activities, which the reader can only surmise must have consisted of more face-to-face confrontations.

Similarly, the Methodist families at Rinsey, near Praa Sands, were known to be active in smuggling. The Carters and Richards made use of the isolated, rocky shoreline at Prussia Cove to bring French rum and brandy ashore; something teetotallers in other societies would have found abhorrent. But it demonstrates that Wesley was dealing with a range of characters from drunkards, lawless wreckers and tinners spoiling for a fight, and his message made no distinction between persons. He was able to persuade and influence and win over the most hardened Cornish heart.

Founding Families
Wesley visited Cornwall for four decades and although there were riots against him, animosity from various clergy and setbacks of a practical nature, there continued to be great pockets of revival. Compelled by Wesley's message men and women would fall to their knees in repentance, often in extreme emotional displays, including sobbing and wailing. Hymns were sung in earnest afterwards and great shouts of joy and exultation would abound as a spontaneous reaction to conversion.

Wesley's brother Charles was a prolific hymn writer and there is no doubt that the words and music were combined to create a rousing and inspirational atmosphere. There would be proclamations of praise through hymn singing, many composed using popular music. They were specifically written to ensure that those who didn't take to studying Christian doctrines easily could remember the essentials through a rousing melody. The lyrics were often introduced first, line by line so the words could be memorised by those who couldn't read. Many illiterate learned to read in this way.

Often there was a large number of inquisitive onlookers who attended open-air meetings and public services. Strong criticism surrounded these gatherings mostly from religious or civic leaders. The conversions were seen to be artificially created and giving way to every kind of excess of emotion. It is perhaps Wesley's special emphasis on living a life of 'holiness' that made his message so unpalatable to some critics.

Many Methodists found they were not welcomed in the established churches so they developed an unmistakable Christian life of their own, meeting together for scripture lessons and hymns. Wesley's group of regular helpers or laymen grew and many gave up secular work to become travelling preachers or itinerants. The itinerant, unpaid Cornish preachers worked within circuits. The ideals of productivity, self-improvement and moral duty were instilled into the Methodist culture.

These laymen were sent to be class leaders with pastoral oversight over members. Some notable names were Peter Jaco, a Newlyn fisherman (1729–1815) and Richard Rodda, a Sancreed Miner (1743–1815). They were said to be a 'Fisher of Men ordained by Christ alone'.

Many mine captain preachers upheld the values of respectability and self-improvement in their ministering messages and this created a culture of honest productivity among the working classes and a subsequent rise in prosperity.

Whole extended families were mindful of Wesley's teachings and carried out their daily lives adhering to his doctrines and principles. There was, generally speaking, a clear distinction between those who were 'Chapel' as opposed to 'Church'.

Many of those who became Methodist preachers in the foundation years were less well educated, speaking in their own dialect, and, as such, townsfolk who were in the professions, or part of the gentry, tended to attend state-affiliated churches as a matter of course.

There was a general assumption that those who followed Wesley's teachings were more earnest and seemingly more pious, having undergone conversion rather than merely being Christian because they had been baptised as an infant. These conversions were dramatic in some cases, with previously notorious drunkards becoming fully reformed characters, taking the pledge of abstinence and going on to live 'God fearing' lives. There are tales that the pit ponies, down the tin mines, no longer worked after their masters were converted; so used were the animals to being cursed and sworn at, that a reformed vocabulary didn't have the same effect.

Throughout his life Wesley and his brother longed to bridge the gap between the Church of England and the growing numbers of new converts. Yet as the Methodist movement grew, the gap appeared instead to widen. Methodism offered a self-contained religion and for many the parish church became unnecessary.

Last Days

When Wesley was coming towards the end of his ministry he was faced with a dilemma that had caused him unease throughout his life's work. In his youth he was uncomfortable about the way Methodism had in many ways separated itself from the mainstream Church of England and he felt some personal responsibility for this. It could be argued that Methodism's success was due to the fact that it had weekday meetings within close-knit societies, but a natural consequence of this was that Societies developed a life of their own within the communities.

Whatever the influences that moulded the denomination, it was Wesley who came to a decisive point. Before his death, Wesley prepared for the work to continue without him. He drew up a list of 100 lay preachers who were to act as a governing body, meeting annually for a Conference. These 'Legal Hundred' would eventually decide to break away from the Church of England even though this was something Wesley strove to avoid. It wasn't until he died in 1791 that moves to disconnect could begin in earnest and a formal separation took place in 1795.

During his later years Wesley became an accepted part of the nation's religious scene. The persecution ceased and Anglican churches became more open, allowing him to preach in their pulpits. Two such pulpits remain in the parish churches at North Tamerton and Week St Mary.

Towns that once hemmed in on him with menacing mobs, considered him to be worthy of deference. By the time he was an old man of eighty-six in 1789 he had won the hearts of the majority. Those who write of him at that time note that as he passed through towns and villages in Cornwall people were hanging out of windows so that they could catch a glimpse of him and shout words of blessing and encouragement.

Such was the impact of Methodism upon the Cornish community that it was not unknown for hymn singing to take place on board boats and down the mines; religious folksongs or ditties were readily accepted among employees as were prayers and readings of scripture.

Socially the Methodist chapels offered dignity to the uneducated; the denomination conferred a sense of seemliness upon those who may have been previously considered ignorant. Certainly the regular exposure to the written words in hymns and scripture meant that many gained a free education and learned to read and write.

Sunday schools offered children a chance to gain basic instruction (compulsory education began in the late 1800s). And because there was such a strong emphasis on self-betterment, many would have turned away from previous activities such as drinking and gambling, as to do so promoted a healthier more prosperous household. Cornwall was also becoming affluent through mining, quarrying and shipping, and many people gained wealth equal to the landowning gentry, but because of their lack of family history they failed to find acceptance in the higher Churches of England. There is no doubt that Wesley tapped into a great social need, he believed in the honouring of all men, however lowly in birth and, as such, influenced a change within Cornish society.

Throughout the 1800s revivals in different towns throughout Cornwall continued to take place and chapels grew and new ones were built. Lay preachers and evangelists continued to walk in Wesley's footsteps, with the same sense of passion and enthusiasm. Certainly the Methodist magazines of 1799 describe gatherings in St Just, Penzance and at Redruth in 1798 when people were said to have been crying out in great agonies of the soul. They were often not comforted until they had purportedly found peace with their maker. At this time 2,000 new members joined Penzance's circuit of societies.

Liskeard's Wesley Methodist Church (1968) was built in 1846. John Wesley passed through the town on many occasions.

Yet despite these increases in chapel attendance there were schisms and rifts among the members that resulted in divisions within the Methodist denomination. Bible Christians, Primitive Methodists, Wesleyan Methodists, United Methodist Free Churches and Methodist New Connexion each had their own specific interpretations concerning doctrinal issues and practice. Without the single autocratic control of Wesley such differences, some of them hardly apparent to the outside eye, were inevitable it seems. All were to reunite eventually in 1932 when there was a general union of all factions. However, the results of these differences are still evident today on the chapel stones and account for the overabundance of chapel buildings in some areas such as Stithians, Temple, Wadebridge and Redruth.

The peak in Cornish Methodist membership occurred between 1840 and 1850; since then the movement has known consistent decline. The movement would never again see the extraordinary expansion as in Wesley's days. Although pockets of revival and consistent chapel attendance were recorded

Camelford Methodists' faith tea in 1941 typifies chapel culture, which is still continued in some measure in chapel coffee mornings nowadays.

in various parts of Cornwall, the initial widespread phenomenon of mass conversion was lost with Wesley's death, it seems.

Victorian Methodism fell into a state of respectability where ideals of industrious activity, sobriety, education and moral decency were the ideological foundations of living. The radical open-air preaching in the byways was replaced by a more seemly religion that made for a more comfortable outworking of the Christian call.

This was a time when those of the middle classes could afford to rent pews in a chapel and there was an apparent division between those that 'had' and those who 'had not'. The poor were segregated to benches at the front and the initial love of the poor that Wesley promoted was lost.

Hymns, prayers and Bible reading with preaching continued as before and are still the pattern of chapel services today. Yet the only time that one can catch a glimpse of the denomination's pioneering origins is at the annual gatherings at Gwennap Pit. It is possible, with imagination, to gain something of the extraordinary ministry of Wesley.

However John Wesley is perceived, whether in reverence or scepticism, there can be no denying that this itinerant preacher man influenced Cornwall's culture. By taking a moment to ponder at one of the hundreds of Methodist places of worship, it is possible to capture an inkling of a deep spirituality within the heart of one man – unique to him in past times, and lost to us, save in the retelling of the tale.

CHAPTER 2

RURAL LIFE

It will bear a shower every week day and two upon a Sunday.
There cannot be too much rain before mid-summer, nor too little after.
Cornish country sayings: *General View of the Agriculture of the County
of Cornwall*, produced for the Board of Agriculture and Internal
Improvement, G.B. Worgan, 1811

Cornwall has a rich agricultural heritage. Without land management and the labour of generations of rural workers, much of the countryside we appreciate today – woodlands, hedges and field systems – would be inaccessible, given over to impenetrable thickets, rough brambles and scrubland.

Harvest time at Porthscatho with views of Gerrans Bay, Nare Head and Bodmin Point taken in 1959. Here the corn harvest has been left in piles to dry for a few days. Each pile is in the required amount for one sheaf, which would then be bound by lengths of twisted straw or twine.

The North Cornwall hounds meet at The Old Inn at St Breward in 1957.
Traditionally farmers welcomed the hunt onto their land, as they kept
foxes at bay and were part of the land-management process.

It is easy to assume that much of the natural landscape has either been carefully tamed or is pretty much as nature intended. But the ruthless clearing and cultivating of land has been taking place since the Iron Age. Brutal burning and felling, then allowing wild native herds to graze and reduce vegetation, made areas manageable for cultivation. Even expansive open fields of grass were a carefully managed crop, a valuable grazing resource that could also be harvested as hay for winter fodder.

Areas generally considered to be 'wild', such as at Bodmin Moor, Pendeen and parts of the Lizard have actually been cleared at some time, grazed, hunted upon and pathways and bridleways established. Very little of what we value in the rural environment, even common land, has been left unmanaged.

The story of Cornish agriculture is in many ways a predictable, gradual replacement of old with new; a way of life passed on from one generation to another. Yet it is also a story of dramatic change in the last 200 years, a change most significantly brought about by mechanisation, the appeal of urban employment, cheaper importation and the social implications wrought by two world wars.

The agricultural industry has seen progress as modern methods have increased production, enabling Cornwall's position to remain competitive in the world market. But as with many progressive practices, this comes at a price, as some ways have had to be forfeited. Much of what used to be 'done by hand', even up until the 1950s, is now achieved in part by modern farm machinery. Mechanised reaping has replaced a community of workers with

Even when this photograph was taken in 1941 haymaking was partly done by hand. The reapers at Tregar, Nanstallon are seen here enjoying croust, which has been brought out to them mid-morning while they work in the fields. Tea poured from enamel pots, with heavy cake or saffron buns, would keep workers going until lunchtime.

scythes and gleaners during harvest time. Sewing of seed, planting of potato crops, harrowing, weeding, bird scaring, and feeding the soil with manure are all carried out by farm machinery, driven by a lone farmer in his cab. Almost all farms today employ the use of chemicals and artificial fertilizers, replacing the need for manual labour.

Nowadays, the management and workload of the farm is the responsibility of one or two managers, run as a business, instead of employing a whole hamlet of farmhands. Machinery has replaced the livelihood of a small village. As a consequence, rural working communities have dispersed, farming families have moved apart and a way of life has been immersed in a tide of change.

What the horse couldn't do in this scene, captured in 1940 on Margate Farm near Bodmin, then manual labour had to. By 1850 mechanised horse-drawn reaping machines were beginning to replace a team of men with scythes (which were used instead of the outdated reaping hooks or sickles). However, the tractor and combine harvester was a rarity until the changeover began in earnest in the late 1950s. This rendered these noble heavy horses nonessential. Old farming skills such as Cornish hedge-building, coppicing, ploughing and reaping using heavy horses or oxen are now almost obsolete skills.

This threshing machine at Penbugle near Bodmin still requires a team of workers but nevertheless was considered to offer labour-saving benefits in 1939.

In surveys written by R. Frazer in 1794, and G.B. Worgan in 1811 for the National Board of Agriculture, attempts were made to examine the working methods of farming in Cornwall at that time. All of the hedging, coppicing, ploughing, harrowing, planting, hoeing and harvesting was carried out by hand or with basic machinery and the help of a team of heavy horses or oxen.

A huge range of hand tools and implements were used, with amusing names such as sneaths, dodgers, crooks, turnip dobbers, nibs and tangs. These were often hand-made for a specific purpose. There were a few wheel ploughs, foot ploughs, and other county ploughs being introduced, and trials made with them; but the old Cornish hand plough still maintained its ground. Thrashing machines, however, were used throughout the Duchy with few farms of consequence being without them, being mostly driven by horses, a few by water, and, uniquely, one by revolutionary steam.

The aims of these government reports were to offer the Cornish farmer strategies for improvement. As Frazer states:

> To contribute his mote to the improvement of the country... not only
> in the valleys, on the sea courts and great general circumstances of
> the county.

Their reports took account of the climate, natural landscape and way of life for farm workers and recommendations were made. They recognised agriculture was a fundamental mainstay of Cornwall's economy. It is from these two documents, of the very few agricultural records which exist, that this chapter identifies some of the influences that have shaped the countryside.

It seems that suggestions for change from agricultural officials were met with some active resistance: the Cornish had their own way of doing things, as this extract reveals. Frazer comments:

> Men of superior wisdom; observing the absolute sway with which
> prejudice seems to govern the rustic practice of an art which is
> capable of receiving so much aid from science, are very apt to lose
> their tempers, and to consider the tenacious observance of accus-
> tomed practices a proof of the want of understanding...
> It seems astonishing, that it is so difficult to persuade them...

At the start of the 1800s Cornwall's agricultural industry was beginning to feel the sting of a reluctance to invest. Mining and all related industry presented a more profitable return and, as such, increasingly attracted business capital from the wealthy. Worgan observed that there was a 'want of capital' and that 'greater encouragement' was needed in the employment of capital, as was found in other branches of business.

The entire process would take 200 years, but the early 1800s marked the beginning of irreversible changes brought about by commercial interests. Farming families going back generations would become displaced, parts of the landscape were changed drastically and rural lifestyles altered beyond recognition, due to the pressures of commerce.

Frazer, however, seemed to dismiss any possibilities that times were hard for some, and took a blinkered approach. He failed to acknowledge wider political influences concerning world trade and commerce. From his comments it is easy to surmise that there had been some degree of complaints regarding Cornwall's rural economy. He firmly refuses to engage in any suggestion that lack of prosperity was anything other than lack of application:

> On the whole, Cornwall's populous, as it is in the mining districts and along the sea coasts, if agriculture was more attended to, there can be no doubt that it would supply subsistence for a much greater population that it actually possesses.
>
> The sea affords ample supplies of a variety of fish, potatoes grow nowhere in greater plenty, or of better quality; by further exertions of industry in cultivating their lands, it will be obvious to any one who views that county, that they may produce grain of all kinds in great abundance, and it is to be hoped, that we shall soon hear no more of complaints of scarcity, or approaching famine, in a country where nature has bestowed so much, and man done so little.

The agricultural officials gave reports concerning the prosperity of the region, in variance to the abject poverty in some homes, insisting new methods would improve the rural economy. Just a few decades later Cornwall went on to suffer from a prolonged recession, from about the 1870s up to the First World War. This was something Frazer and Worgan were not able to foresee. Frazer's and Worgan's reports are innocent of the trouble ahead. They portray no sense of foreboding and their tone is full of optimism for a bright and ambitious future. On the other hand, it seems that the farmers themselves were beginning to sense the trouble ahead by the general complaints being voiced to officialdom.

However, Frazer does acknowledge the conflict and uprisings in mining areas regarding the export of grain, particularly barley from Cornwall, which directly affected miners. Wheat was grown for bread and for staple human food, barley for brewing and for making poor man's barley bread, oats for porridge and livestock.

Frazer reports that there were some local farmers at Fowey, Padstow and St Germans who were finding it easier, and just as profitable, to allow Cornish grain to be sold to merchants for export (mostly to Spain). It saved them the arduous journeys to markets 'up country'. This in turn led to demands for some supplies to be held back for the mining districts, where grain wasn't being grown in such quantities. It wasn't possible for them to be self-sufficient as in other areas of the Duchy, as much land was given over to industrial use. But Frazer is scathing of the tinners' need for cheap bread and considers them to be unlawful in their activities to fight for reform. Hoards of tinners regularly made their way to places of exportation, such as Falmouth Docks, to openly negotiate with merchant traders. They desperately wanted to deter the merchants from exporting much-needed supplies. Cornwall began to see a pace of change in its agricultural history as the unstoppable surge towards overseas trade began.

This situation was far from straightforward. It was not just the export of grain that caused tensions, but the import of foodstuffs, too. The Corn Laws (in force between 1815 and 1846) were a series of statutes intended to keep corn prices high, restricting the influx of cheaper imported grain. Landowners and farming gentry throughout Cornwall and the British Isles had a vested interest in seeing that these laws were enforced. Tenant farmers also relied on the corn harvest to pay their landlord's rents.

By the 1820s the working classes living in urban areas were spending all their wages on grain products for bread, a basic survival food, which left little over for other goods. This had dire consequences for all urban businesses and prevented economic growth in the manufacturing industry. Opposition from the merchant classes grew, with strong demands being made for the lifting of restrictions on corn price fixing. The gentry began to lose their influence in Parliament to a new kind of business elite, whose concerns were focussed on urban manufacturing industries. This led in 1828 to the first of the Corn Law reforms, which allowed free trade and cheap imported foodstuffs on a sliding scale. Wool began to make its way from America and Australia over the next four decades. British farmers could no longer compete with lower grain, wool and meat prices and their local trade suffered as a consequence. In addition, there followed several years of bad weather resulting in poor harvests and widespread disease.

These were the beginnings of economic depression, most significant between 1860 and 1914. Many landowners could not afford to maintain their buildings. Tenant farmers increasingly had to brave poverty as buildings and land fell into disrepair, creating a sense of despair for the future. Certain rural areas suffered squalid and semi-derelict living conditions.

The *West Briton* newspaper in 1843 reported that high rents, taxes and heavy rates precipitated the departure of 280 rural workers from the village of Stratton for Plymouth, to take up prospects overseas, a situation indicative of the times. Young men took the opportunity, leaving their parents and grandparents behind, to emigrate.

Yeoman farmers downsized to become smallholders; some survived, others didn't. These hardy farming folk were used to physical exertion, and put in long hours to sustain a basic living. But to do so they needed to improvise and be inventive in unpredictable times. Mining and manufacturing industries offered employment for many cottagers, taking them away from a farming livelihood that up until then had been the main source of wealth for the most influential in society.

In many ways, until this time, working the land had remained consistent with traditional, manual farming methods used for centuries. Yet cheaper imports, faster shipping transportation and a change in consumer demands all led to the decline of the 'family farm' principle, based on support from family and neighbours. This traditional close-knit community is now close to extinction in the twenty-first century. Gone are the days when whole extended families worked alongside each other, digging, ditching, gathering the harvest. Such collective farming practices have been replaced by more efficient farming methods and occasional hired labour, rather than a year-round full-time working community.

The Lie of the Land

When faced with one of Cornwall's numerous tranquil and inspirational scenic views today, it is hard to grasp the amount of heartache and crisis that has inevitably accompanied each acre. Many farmers, in the last century in particular, had to cope with turbulent times, European legislation, safety regulations and bureaucracy. The farmer today, although pushing forward with new scientific methods and coping with political challenges unique to our time, still relies on the principles of land management and husbandry from the past, adapting what their forefathers already achieved.

Only by looking at the past can we ascertain how we have perhaps reached today's position in rural Cornwall. An understanding of why land is apportioned, and for what purpose buildings and boundaries were constructed, gives us insight into our environmental context. It brings greater depth of appreciation of those in the past who laid the foundations of what we inherited. The farm cottages, barns, stiles, gateposts and field patterns can in many ways be easily overlooked, their significance forgotten and ignored. Yet these physical structures stand as signs and act as reminders.

There can be little argument that Cornwall's natural beauty has been threatened by the demands of an increasing population with all its materialistic needs. The influx of visitors began when the railway was finished in 1852, opening Cornwall up to the rest of Britain. With the completion of Brunel's Tamar bridge, also in 1852, more seasonal tourists ventured over the river and a new holiday industry was born. Despite the many copses, ancient land-marks, winding byways and historic buildings that still remain, whole swathes of Cornish farmland have been altered or lost for good.

The term 'progress' is used spuriously to justify decades of development around villages and rural towns, until we are faced with a confused, hap-hazard mix of retirement homes, holiday accommodation and seasonal venues to feed and entertain the tourist.

Industrial parks have spread into out-of-town locations, surrounded by fields, and accepted by planners because of economic necessity. Housing estates, road networks and the relentless flow of traffic, overhead wires and cables, commercial centres with all the paraphernalia of an electronic age (manufacturing and industrial ages before that) have all contributed to the loss of rural ways of life.

Seaside towns, Newquay, Perranporth, Praa Sands, Portreath and Hayle, in particular, have seen bungalows, hotels and garages, cafés and road networks begin to dominate what only a century and a half ago would have been remote coastal or rural locations.

It is easy to become nostalgic when looking back, even just a few decades, imagining it was somehow better 'back then' in some 'golden era'. Undoubtedly the countryside has changed and aspects have disappeared for-ever, but it can become problematic to idealise previous times, hankering after aspects we assume made for a better life.

The 'good old days' weren't immune to disease or unpredictable weather. Cumbersome farming and domestic practices, although effective in their way, were nevertheless reliant on the vigour and resilience of a skilled workforce. If a crop failed or the weather spoiled a harvest, the whole community suffered, poverty ensued and with that the standard of living dropped for all in the vicinity.

Certainly rural workers have always lived lives far from the 'picture perfect' idyll easily conjured up by a collection of old photographs. The reality of life on the land was always labour-intensive; it was the hardy who survived.

Working with Nature

This picture of a bounteous crop of turnips at Trewashford, St Mellion, was used as a fertiliser advert in 1908. The heavy farm horse and cart was an integral part of farm life and a valuable asset.

Since earliest times, working the land has been a fight with the elements, respecting nature's supremacy yet plundering its provision. The farmer's relationship with the environment has necessitated submission to that which is unchangeable, the geological and lie of the land, general wind direction and climate.

A farmer's decisions, when surveying a plot, recognised the need to harness benefits that were naturally supplied, such as water sources and soil conditions, respecting the fact that natural forces have the capacity to take over and negate human endeavours.

Frazer identified various soil types in Cornwall (it is predominantly acid) but records: 'so great is the variety of soil in the county of Cornwall, that to describe it with correctness, would require a history of every parish.'

In some respects nature has the ascendancy, bearing her influence upon all that has been claimed for human use. Extreme weather, pests and diseases, as well as uncultivated vegetation encroaching upon crops, are all part of the farmer's struggle.

Worgan, in his 1811 report, describes how crops can fail to thrive in coastal regions, being blighted by their situation, as they, 'sustain much injury from violence of Westerly wind and salt spray off the sea... hence

A team of heavy horses pulling a cart stacked with sacks of grain in 1914. On these crossroads between Tregony and Truro a motorcar would have been a rare sight. It wasn't until the 1920s that the motorist began to frequent the lanes of Cornwall.

crops of wheat and turnips have been totally destroyed.'

Cornwall is renowned for its natural landscape and is a place of much contradiction and diversity. In parts there are the almost hostile moorlands, such as are found at St Agnes Beacon, Carn Brea, Carnmenellis and Trencrom Hill, with their bleak granite outcrops, the odd wind-stunted tree, and hill-sides covered with gorse and heather. Blackthorn and hawthorn survive the driving coastal winds, along with bracken and a few other hardy hedgerow plants embedded in sheltered crevices between granite-walled hedges.

When Worgan writes about Cornwall's landscape it is at a time when few roads would take a carriage:

> ... remarkable for inequality of surface; ascents and descents follow in rapid succession. Some of the hills are very steep, and tediously prolong a journey. The great post-roads being carried many miles together, over rugged, naked, and uncultivated heaths and moors, the traveller is impressed with a more unfavourable opinion of the county than it deserves.

It is somewhat ironic that today these remote moorlands draw so many visitors to the region. It is the 'over rugged' landscape that makes Cornwall such a popular destination for those seeking respite from urban pressures.

As late as the nineteenth century, pedestrians, farm carts and the occasional horse and carriage would have been all that frequented the country lanes of the Duchy.

Walking was the main means of visiting a neighbouring farmstead and the meandering lanes and dusty tracks were pounded into permanence by the endless driving of livestock.

The mass production of bicycles in the 1890s made enormous savings of time for the farm labourer. But so unusual were cars that an article in the *West Briton* newspaper in 1897 reported that there had been a motorcar in Cornwall, which had been met by hundreds of people lining the streets to look at the spectacle. It wasn't until the 1920s, when more motorists started to come down to Cornwall, that tarmacadam roads were established to facilitate the influx of traffic, although cars were still a rarity and not generally commonplace until the 1950s. This in turn opened up the marketing trade of livestock and crops, enabling greater ease of transportation with farm trucks and lorries. The impact on a typical village was marked, as livestock were no longer free to roam.

Motorists today negotiate winding narrow lanes between high, banked hedges that were only ever intended for the occasional solitary horse and cart, or for driving a herd of pigs to market. It is rare now to come across a tranquil backwater without hearing the drone of traffic in the distance.

Along Cornwall's North Coast road one is reminded of the hardships experienced by farmers and fishermen sustaining a livelihood from sea and land, pitted against the elements, exposed to storms and sea mists that envelop the wild terrain whatever the season. Worgan noticed that, 'trees and shrubs shrink and lean away to the eastward and appear as if clipped by gardener's shears.'

It is hard to envisage, when stood in these isolated and almost desolate moors, with trees bent by the relentless assault from Atlantic winds, that just a few miles inland towards the southern coast a kinder vista awaits.

Stretching along the South Coast the climate is kinder, with sheltered districts inland from Falmouth, St Just in Roseland and St Germans benefiting from sub-tropical temperatures, very occasional frosts and milder coastal conditions. On these lowland river valleys, palm trees thrive and rare species of imported plants have established a home.

Deciduous woodland and a rich array of plant and fauna compliment green pastureland, typifying the idyllic pastoral scene. Hedgerows of dogrose, elder, hazel and holly contain an extensive variety of wildflowers, including primrose, violet, wild honeysuckle and red campion. Worgan encouraged his fellow government officials to take the time to explore more temperate lowland areas:

> But he who will traverse, imbibe different ideas of the general features of the county, which in many parts, he will find pleasingly broken into hill and dale; some of the valleys are beautifully picturesque, and richly diversified with corn, woods, coppices, orchards, running waters, and verdant meadows.

Today, gardens have been created and are open to the public. They enthusiastically celebrate the temperate growing conditions at Heligan, Trebah, Glendurgan, Trelissick, Trengwainton and, more recently, the world-renowned Eden Project.

In these clement areas, today's farmer also benefits from an early spring and longer growing seasons; daffodils and narcissi crops gain pre-eminence across many rural views during late January and February.

These women employed in seasonal flower picking on the Isles of Scilly (1922), are harvesting by hand, as pickers still do today. However, plastic crates are now used instead of these hand-woven baskets. Today bunches of narcissi or daffodils can be dispatched to any county on the mainland in a matter of hours.

Perhaps some would assume that seed-time and harvest are predictable, timeless cycles, although with modern intensive methods, even the growing seasons have been circumvented. Potato crops and strawberries can be tricked into earlier propagation than might be achieved naturally, using clear plastic sheeting as insulation from an occasional frost. From a distance it looks like field upon field of freshly fallen snow. Because of milder winters south of the River Tamar, and the insulating plastic covers, Cornish cauliflower, early potatoes and broccoli are able to make it into the shops weeks before competitors outside the Duchy.

Ancient Times

Since the Iron Age, Cornish settlers have claimed the wild wasteland for livestock and crops. It was from this period that the most significant and singularly important change to the landscape began – tree clearance. As the natural woodland began to be cleared, acre by acre, a way was made for domesticated crops and animal husbandry.

This clearing process was still under way during Frazer's time and he describes how it was done:

> The process they pursue is, in general by paring and burning the surface of the ground. The land is then dressed with ashes, and a compost of sea sand, earth and the scrapings of lanes, in which they add dung which they save in the farmyard.

The light black earth, which is found beneath the heathland or Cornish furze, is intermixed with small gravel. Frazer wrote that this type of soil was called growan.

Field patterns have had their boundary lines influenced by geological features and in some areas remain unchanged since earliest times. They are enclosed by granite and slate outcrops, and man-made earth banks or ditches. The boulders are often so big that it would be almost impossible to remove them from where they are situated. They were therefore left as permanent features and indisputable boundary markers by the early Celts.

Some of the hedges date back 6,000 years and Cornwall has an estimated 30,000 miles of unique stone-faced hedge-banks; earth banks contained by granite walls. Bushes and trees cling to the top. These provided the early settlers with natural animal enclosures, or were used as sheltered plots, protected from the coastal winds, suited to growing crops such as oats or rye.

But interpreting any farmland usage requires the informed eye, and a range of expertise is needed to decipher the complexities behind a rural site. The development of the Cornish countryside is not as straightforward as it initially may appear. Sometimes the clues to the past are obscure, perhaps only a discovered item or the crumbling foundations of a wall. Sometimes there are minimal marks left on a landscape, just slight inclines or minor changes in soil types. Often it needs an expert archeologist by aeroplane to analyse a stretch of the countryside and decipher obscure imprints, sometimes only visible from above. These hidden patterns lie beneath turf and ploughed soil.

Although many of the villages and landscaping we see today are predominantly the product of the last 1,500 years of farming, there are clear indications, specifically in Cornwall, that many farms were possibly rebuilt on original Celtic sites. Although it remains to be proven beyond doubt that some farmsteads have been inhabited continuously since Celtic times, it seems likely that many have.

West Cornwall has some of Britain's finest examples of early farming settlements and ancient field boundaries around St Buryan, Carn Euny and Chysauster in Penwith. By walking up the hill from Lamorna along the Pilgrim's Way towards the Merry Maidens stone circle, examples of ancient boundary markers can be seen as part of the hedge-bank system.

Worgan visited West Cornwall for part of his survey and was struck by what he saw:

> The admirers of sublime scenery, will be highly gratified to behold stupendous rocks, which form great barriers against the ocean, particularly about Lands End and Lizard, filling the mind with awe, and giving rise to these solemn and sublime sensations, which elevate the heart to an almighty all-creating power.

The Iron Age site at Carn Euny, on a clear day, looks out across the Land's End peninsula to the coast with the Scilly Isles just beyond sight. Gorse, turf, granite moor stones, stunted trees and a few isolated cottages are the main features on this moorland.

The foundation-stones of a village of ten roundhouses has a few human details to catch the eye. Rooms, windows and doorways, a fireplace, cobbled floor and grinding stones have all been excavated and are clearly defined although incomplete. It is a place where we can begin to identify with our forefathers. Here lived ancient communities that ceased to pursue a nomadic way, choosing instead to live sedentary lifestyles based more on cultivation.

Hunter-gatherers, who would have traditionally followed herds of wild deer and cattle, foraging for edible plants, began to master the skills of domesticating enclosed livestock.

The layout of the village gives a tangible insight into how early settlers organised themselves to survive off the land. It is easy to envisage the original Cornish smallholder and stockbreeder in a small village, keeping livestock and growing some native crops to feed the community. Here are the homes of Cornwall's founding farmers.

It is likely that subsequent generations of farmers recognised the benefits of small enclosures on difficult terrain. They provide much-needed shelter from coastal winds so would have kept these original sites agriculturally active, maintaining what was already established. Some enclosures have remained in constant use and the shapes of fields have rarely changed since their initial foundation.

In Penwith there has been consistency and continuity in the use of the land since earliest times. On this and other ancient Celtic sites, it can seem at a fleeting glance, as if little has changed in rural Cornwall.

Domestic Arrangements

In Worgan's report on the homes of farm workers there seems to be little to differentiate them from early Celtic buildings. Obviously, at some point the round-walled designs were replaced by cornerstones and straight walls, and an upper floor was added. Yet, there were still striking similarities between what is recorded in 1811 and what archeologists believe living conditions were like for Celtic inhabitants.

In 1811 descriptions of farms and property present a rural design in building that has been consistent in many ways throughout the ages, reliant on natural stone, built by hand, crafted using basic tools and focused around hearth, food production and livestock welfare. It is a simple rural architecture that has prevailed and can be identified in many of our historical and listed buildings.

Worgan notes that many agricultural workers' cottages had several rooms. However, they still had wheaten straw or reed-thatched roofs and, commonly, earthen floors. Archeologists have surmised that the Celts also used thatch and similar building materials. Some of the dwellings at Carn Euny were constructed from the plentiful supply of flagstones for flooring. This practice is commonplace in rural cottages throughout Cornwall, the ground floor being of flag, the upper rooms of oak. It is profound that so little changed in rustic building for so many centuries, reflecting a way of life that, in many ways, remained consistent until the First World War.

The Duchy, perhaps because of its remote location, or maybe because of the permanence of some of the boundary walls, was hardly affected by the widespread apportioning of land by 'piecemeal' by medieval lords throughout England. Colonisation of the Cornish countryside took place gradually over the centuries, an organic process, not formally designed, but one driven by communal need.

It seems likely that early farming villages were initially several isolated farmsteads, located at walking distance from one another. Hamlets would have spread out as a spontaneous response to growing populations and depended on the availability and viability of nearby agricultural land.

This pattern of building was based on communal living and mutual co-operation, crucial for all rural workers in the past. This meant that rows of cottages were built alongside the main thoroughfare or in clusters around a central area. The skills of blacksmiths, weavers, thatchers, millers and hedge-layers were all required, as were the seasonal vagrants who travelled from farm to farm at busy times, gaining a meal and a dry barn to sleep in where they could. The church, shop, doctor and vet were all there to serve the agricultural population.

The quintessential Cornish cottage that epitomises rural life is typified by the thatched roof, cob walls, hand-hewn timbers, cottage-style garden with hollyhocks, honeysuckle and herbs. Today idealised versions are reproduced on greeting cards and fudge boxes, but the realities of living under thatch when there was no money to pay for repairs must have been grim. This extract from Worgan's report was intended to highlight the plight of some agricultural workers at that time. Although he was obviously describing buildings in disrepair, by including these details he was hoping to procure some capital for the regions' farms:

> I had occasion often, in my dreary walks, to take shelter in some miserable dwellings, and found the poor inhabitants busy in placing their bowls, crocks and pans, to catch the waters pouring in at the roof.

In his report Worgan starts to recommend the use of slate tiles instead of the wheaten or reed thatch, which was the norm for all living accommodation. Here we see the beginnings of a change that would decimate the trade of the thatcher and transform the aesthetics of almost every rural village.

But it was not only the thatcher whose livelihood suffered; the hedge-layer's skills were no longer required as Victorian farmers began to make use of newly invented barbed wire, which not only saved time in creating new animal enclosures but also reduced burdensome labour costs. Barbed wire was a cheap alternative to paying a hedger for the repair of tumbling banks.

The report differentiated between several types of farm worker. The resident yeoman farmer leased the main farmhouse from the estate, where the landowner may or may not have lived in a manor house or farm nearby. The yeoman would be responsible for all the land management; maintaining buildings and hiring labour, either resident farm servants or apprentice workers from the village. These apprentices were often orphans, cared for by the parish, whose only chance of survival was to find employment that provided board and lodging.

Prior to a series of education acts that came into force in late-Victorian times, children in farming families were often fully employed as bird scarers, or set to work alongside the women, weeding, hoeing and gleaning at harvest time. Women did work on the land during busy times, but in general it was culturally deemed to be preferable for them to be domestically occupied.

They were actively involved in animal husbandry close to the house. Along with the laundry, butter- and cheese-making, bread-baking and meal preparation, it was ever the case that sick or birthing livestock needed to be attended to. Chickens needed to be fed, and goats, and a domestic cow or two had to be milked. On average, during these times, women had an estimated ten pregnancies in a lifetime, although not all mothers and infants survived.

The main farmhouse could be of considerable size, with a large common kitchen and living area where all the family, farm servants and daily hired help would eat together. There were often two rooms on the ground floor, including a parlour, although farm labourers only ever ate in the kitchen. All the daily domestic chores were focused around the fire or, in later years, the range, which was fuelled by turf, furze, coppiced wood or shipments of Welsh coal.

The fire burned continuously and the main meal was usually stewed in a cauldron. It consisted mainly of potatoes, rabbit and seasonal vegetables, accompanied by barley bread or wheaten loaves baked on a covered hot plate or in a bread oven. In more prosperous farmsteads a little home-slaughtered meat could be afforded. Larger cuts of meat were thrust on a spit and turned over an open fire or roasted in the oven.

Apple pies, heavy cakes and saffron buns were also enjoyed when visitors arrived, although sugar had to be bought for these. On feast days and at harvest time, plum pudding, apple dumplings, cream cheese, cider and beer were used to celebrate, along with songs and dancing. This hearth-focused approach to family living seems to have been the norm in the less prosperous tenant houses, too.

Basic cottage buildings were made of mud and cob walls, or later from granite blocks. In places such as Launceston, where slate was readily available, it was used to clad the cottage, acting as added weatherproofing.

Some rural homes, it seems, had a cellar, dairy room or pantry added to the one large common room, or a two smaller-roomed layout. The ceilings were uncommonly low and floors were of earth, lime ash or flagstone. The walls would have been covered in lime or whitewash. Upstairs there were bedchambers, with floorboards and often open eaves with exposed thatch.

Outside there may have been a porch, pig-house, 'bog room' and a water-supply – either a stream or a well with a pump. It was part of the women's work to continually fetch water from the well in clone pitchers (a type of pot). By the mid-twentieth century most Cornish farms had a supply of running water and this meant the arduous task of carrying buckets back and forth from the pump or well, for domestic animals and the household, was no longer a relentless task.

More importantly, however, the cottage needed adequate an garden and orchards to keep the family self-sufficient in fruit and vegetables. Outbuildings included hog sheds and chicken houses, providing the occasional supply of meat. The pig was traditionally slaughtered in the autumn and salted ready for the winter months. However, thanks to the close proximity of most hamlets to the sea, there was always a ready supply of salted pilchards and fresh fish.

Outside in the farmyard, close to the house, there would be a feeding place for sheep and oxen where farmhands began their daily routine. Troughs for turnips had to be kept replenished and cribs or racks of hay or straw kept supplied from the fodder house or barn during winter months.

Working the Land

The daily schedule for the labourers was a continual treadmill of tasks. Herds of livestock would need to be driven to a water source twice daily; obviously if a stream or river made this unnecessary then there was one less job to be done. There was fresh grazing to move them on to, dung to clear, feeds to prepare and the sick and breeding animals to attend to. On arable land the seasonal cycle of tasks meant there was little opportunity for respite.

The only time away from the farm was the weekly trips to market, which meant driving the livestock on foot, or when the roads improved in the late 1800s, on the back of a horse and cart. The main sheep fairs were at Summercourt, Mitchell and St Lawrence, with early lambs at Camelford.

*Old Cardinham Sheep Market in 1940. Often these gatherings would be
organised in a field with hay bales as the only enclosures for the livestock.*

The principal cattle fairs were at Bodmin, Grampound, Probus, St Lawrence
and Launceston.

In many ways Frazer and Worgan were observing the start of industrial
change and they were eager to introduce time-saving methods, encouraging
the benefits of scientific initiatives. To them the land of Cornwall presented
a welcome opportunity, being rich in natural resources, but also giving them
scope to introduce their visionary improvements including mechanised
implements, crop rotation and leaving land fallow, and improving living
conditions for workers.

On reading their suggestions one can't help but question the over-
confidence of their tone. Considering that they also noted how the farmers
were already mastering the land themselves, with ingenuity – albeit uncon-

Selling sheep at Wadebridge Market, 1939.

ventionally in some places – it appears that the expert, Frazer, couldn't persuade the Cornish to give up their old-time methods straight away:

> The plough commonly used is extremely awkward and inconvenient. The Suffolk plough, with two horses, without a driver, is used in Trelawn and some other places, and performs double the work, and at much less expense than the common Cornish plough. But farmers will not be persuaded to adopt it.

Both men noticed how turnips were introduced as a crop to improve the soil, something that today we know increases the nitrogen content, adding to fertility.

There are numerous comments in both reports highlighting the ingenious methods used to overcome the tricky terrain, particularly the use of packhorse, mule or ass. For muck spreading, the animal was set up with dung pots, two barrels strung over its back. The dung was carried to the field and released from the pots in small amounts, via a door on the bottom, as the animal trudged back and forth. 'They are indispensable conveyances on the hilly ground,' Worgan commented.

There were many practices that were part of the Cornish way of doing things. Seaweed, sand, as well as bruised and decayed pilchards, were used as soil conditioners and dressings for the land. A farming tip in the *West Briton* in 1844 suggests taking a board that has been freshly painted with tar, and passing it four times a day over a crop of turnips to catch turnip flies.

Harrowing was carried out by a smaller breed of horse, which was favoured by the Cornish because it was lightweight, so could travel faster than the heavy plodding cobs seen elsewhere. A boy would mount one of the two horses, keep them both going at a light trot while harrowing up roots and weeds at a cracking speed. The other workers would then rake up the debris and the lot would be burnt in half a day, a pace that astounded the observer.

Sledges, and not carts, were used to overcome the inaccessibility of some farm tracks, although the packhorse was used for almost everything. Because of the isolation of many farms, the transport difficulties discouraged dairy farming, as it would have been impossible to keep milk fresh while covering such distances. Farms kept cows for domestic use only. It wasn't until the railway was built in 1859 that the transport of fresh milk was made more feasible, to Plymouth and beyond, and dairy farming became a viable livelihood.

Bulb growers on the Scilly Isles and farmers with early crops near Marazion also benefited from the railway, as their crops made it to Covent Garden and a new market was opened up to them.

In the 1800s, farmers began in earnest to take up the breeding and rearing of sheep for wool and mutton, and cattle for beef. The native, hardy, small black cattle, descendants of the livestock of Celtic tribes, thrived on the less verdant, higher ground, although the red Devon breeds were popular because they fattened up quickly.

Potatoes were the main crop, because of the warm climate and moist conditions. This was a mainstay and still is today, even, it was noted, to the point that two crops were planted in a year. They planted Kidney potatoes at Christmas or a few weeks before, which were picked in May, then planted Apple potatoes in the same ground.

When both agricultural experts concluded their reports, there were many favourable and optimistic notes. It seems they anticipated that by following the few commendations, any regional difficulties could be righted with ease. Frazer notes:

> Cornwall possesses the happy advantage of the numerous and public spirited body of gentlemen, who are alive to their native county. The people of Cornwall also possess a great degree of perspicacity

*This Cornish homestead, photographed in 1904, illustrates a typical
smallholding or tenant farm at that time. Note how galvanised steel
has started to replace thatch on the outbuildings.*

and acumen; they attend to new improvements: if they find them
successful, they are not slow in imitation.

They could not have possibly been mindful of the rapidity and enormity of
change that would transform farming in the following century. These
changes, seen in the 1900s in particular, were of great benefit in many ways,
easing the farmer's lot and alleviating some of the burden.

More than a century after Worgan's first recommendations for slate tiles,
farms saw the introduction of galvanised steel as a roofing material for barns
and animal sheds. This also bought with it widespread redundancies in the
thatching trade. Although smaller farms could not afford the initial outlay for
covering barns and hayricks with this new labour-saving material, nevertheless by the 1950s the majority of farm buildings used metal roofing sheets
rather than reed or rush thatch. Dutch barns, constructed from steel and cor-
rugated iron, replaced the resplendent high-roofed, timbered barn, which in

some cases dated back to medieval times. However, old-style barns were also costly to demolish, which is why so many have remained to be converted as residential premises.

Despite its ugliness, concrete, once introduced, created a more sanitised environment inside animal pens and sheds and outside in yards. Previously, attempts were made to create a cobbled or slate base but the farmyard was a notoriously muddy bog of animal dung. It was made worse by wet weather and the continual traffic of hooves and heavy boots churning up the ground. With a fresh water-supply and a yard surface that could be scrubbed down daily, the farmyard became a healthier place. The use of concrete was officially enforced on some farms to safeguard the milk supply and ensure it didn't become contaminated by slurry.

Household sanitation, in some cases only introduced in the 1950s, meant that the outside visits to earth-pit closets, or even the open moors, were no longer necessary, and as hygiene improved so did the health of the community. Typhus, diphtheria, pneumonia and infant mortality were ever-present threats, the realities of which erode any sense of 'old world' charm or romantic appeal that we may have for domestic conditions in the past.

There could be no greater benefit to the farmer than that of electricity. Oil-lamps, which had minimal benefits on a windy, stormy night out of doors, and were liable to create a very real fire risk to hayricks and barns, became a thing of the past. With the introduction of electric lighting in farm buildings, caring for animals, milking and feeding could be done in relative ease whatever the hour of day.

During both world wars petrol-driven tractors, combine harvesters and milking machines were still a rarity. It wasn't until the late 1950s and early 1960s that their use became widespread. It was during the wars that the lack of a large male workforce across the nation caused a crisis and the government activated several initiatives to encourage Cornish farmers to provide food for the nation, using women as the main labouring resource. The lack of human labour after the Second World War led to mechanisation and the adoption of intense growing methods. These two wars accelerated change at a speed that Frazer and Worgan could not have imagined in their time.

Likewise, it is not always possible for us to imagine what life was like in Cornwall in their time. But through their descriptions one is able to piece together a sense of rural life and identify aspects that have survived the passage of time.

Part of some buildings they describe, the traditions, tools and artifacts

*Carn Euny, near Lands End an ancient Celtic settlement with original
foundations of animal enclosures and round houses.*

may have remained, but their full significance may have been lost. Village
pumps, stone mounting blocks, granite slabs by stiles (used to rest coffins
from farm to cemetery) are all clues to and permanent features of the past,
but now functionally redundant.

It is not always possible to 'read' what has been left by previous generations. The archeological evidence can be sparse, corroded, decayed and barely
visible, requiring closer examination and leading to research that may be
inconclusive.

In many respects we are left with gaps in our knowledge and what we piece together can be mere conjecture, with much of the past shrouded in mystery. Yet despite this, a tangible impression from the past can still be gained, maybe not entirely accurate or precise, but a close enough picture. Despite some parts of farming history having been buried under ploughed soil, it is still possible to catch a glimpse of what has disappeared, and there lies the source of endless fascination.

CHAPTER 3

MINING

✳

Tinners have a significant place in the Cornish heritage. All that now remains of their powerful contribution to local culture are the countless grey, redundant stone and red-brick engine houses and mine buildings scattered across the countryside.

Standing on top of Carn Brea near Pool and Redruth it is possible to see from St Agnes Beacon to the north-east along the entire North Coast to St Ives Bay and beyond. From here the extensive influence of mining is evident. All around, ruins of engine houses and chimneys stand out against the landscape. The distinct outlines of their derelict forms are magnificent yet poignant. Here was the centre of Cornwall's mining industry.

Wheal Francis mining area 2007. Standing on the summit of Carn Brea the urban and natural landscape is stretched out towards the North Coast. This was the centre of mining industrialisation and remnants of the past are peppered across the view.

At one time several tens of chimney stacks would have belched out pungent smoke across the nearby towns and surrounding villages. The mineral railways would have been active, including the vital Portreath Tramway, which transported ore from the mines to the sailing vessels waiting at the harbour side. Thousands of men endured punishing conditions and pitted their will and physical strength against the inherent dangers of the mines.

Standing on the granite outcrop next to Carn Brea Castle, there is a vantage point of the landscape, which also gives an insight into mining's past. From a distance, South Crofty Mine appears to be occupied, its headgear rising high above all surrounding buildings, a monument to engineering excellence, looking as if work is still going on. There was almost continuous mining at 'Crofty' for more than 400 years. Starting as a small sett (an opencast pit) in the 1500s, it grew to incorporate other small mines until in 1854 the conglomerate was named South Wheal Crofty. There are an estimated 50 miles of tunnels in the mysterious and now closed-off underground world.

Yet it was as recent as 6 March 1988 that the miners left their last shift, the continuous pump stopped its labours in the engine house and the mine was flooded beyond redemption. Tunnels up to 380 fathoms (695 metres) deep, spanning a number of miles, were filled with water to the adit (drainage) level.

From Carn Brea's elevation it is possible to get a sense of mining's significance and the profound impact it must have had on the entire community.

Dolcoath Mine, Camborne in 1900. This view is now altered beyond recognition. The whole area has been transformed and is clearly visible from Carn Brea. All the mine workings have been cleared apart from the occasional chimney stack.

So many hundreds of thousands of people were connected to the industry in some capacity or other. The enormity of change to each town, brought about by a huge population influx in the 1800s, is permanent, fixed in the slate and granite architecture of row upon row of miners' cottages.

South Crofty's presence can also be seen from the road running through Tuckingmill and Pool. Towns in its shadow carry on despite its demise, bravely facing a future with still-vivid memories of a time when it was the working focus of the entire region.

Now all of the mines' workings have gone. In their place there are industrial parks and superstores, sprawling across converted acres of once-heaped mounds of mining waste. Residents have been left to make sense of the inevitable boom-bust cycle and workers face a different bleakness – unemployment.

Tourists often avoid contact with this mining heartland, as they make their way down the A30 to the coast. Yet this is an undeniable aspect of Cornwall's past. Ugly it may be to face the demise of an industry, to stand and take in the enormity of what has been lost. The landscape is unusually bleak here and depressed times have created a pervading sense of melancholy.

Redruth town was a thriving centre of commerce in the mid-1800s.

Fore Street, Redruth, 1905. At this time the town was still alive with suppliers of goods to mines throughout the world. All the services supplying Cornish mines before the industrial recession still remained in the area, sending their goods to 'Cousin Jacks' overseas.

Traders of all kinds with services for practical needs prospered. Helmets, candles, boots and lanterns were manufactured for the men going underground. Affluent bankers, mine captains, engineers and wealthy businessmen frequented the town streets. Redruth's high, grand buildings endure even though the widespread prosperity the town once enjoyed has departed. Here, expertise that led the mining world was gained. Techniques were mastered by the Cornish miner and his skills were sought after across the globe.

Redruth today struggles on in the face of adversity. The same tenacious resilience found in miners is outworked now in new initiatives and business enterprise. However, despite the cheerful shop fronts and determination to persevere, the streets and alleys portray decades of poverty.

These miners were fighters: fighters against rock, dust, extreme temperatures; fighters against the earth itself. Despite the grieving for loss of a way of life experienced by many families, there is also hope that the tenacious fighting spirit will endure and overcome.

At the start of the Industrial Revolution of the nineteenth century, Cornish tin was at the height of its demand. Prospecting adventurers came down from 'up country' in pursuit of prosperity and capitalist gain. Tin is usually assumed to have been the main metal mined in Cornwall, but copper carried a predominantly greater significance in the eighteenth and nineteenth centuries. The mining of copper and tin are inextricably linked, with deposits of tin being discovered in levels below the previous copper workings. Other, lesser minerals were also sought, such as lead, zinc, nickel, cobalt, silver, tungsten and iron.

Arsenic was originally the foul by-product associated with tin mineralisation, as tin ore was roasted to remove impurities. Later, tin processing involved salvaging arsenic through a complex system of flues. Between 1815 and 1950 arsenic production was crucial to Cornwall's mining economy, the majority of it being used in insecticides and weedkillers. Although a deadly poison, there were very few deaths connected to its production in Cornwall.

It would be easy to assume that tin is a worthless metal from the way we associate it with everyday objects such as tin cans and tin sheds. It is, however, an extremely valuable resource, as small quantities of tin give a corrosive-free surface to cheaply produced iron or steel. The tin-plating industry employed this stable element in the mass production of food containers, though more recently, plastics and aluminum are used in its place.

By the 1850s there were an estimated 50,000 men mining copper and tin. Cornwall was the main international supplier of copper and, as such, provided two-thirds of the entire world's bulk. But while the shareholders and landowners, mine captains and financiers may have benefited from the industrial economic boom, the miners themselves saw fairly modest return for their labour.

Long, punishing shifts in dark and steamy cavernous tunnels, with barely a moment's respite from the discomfort of dusty air, these men were not expected to live beyond 40. Theirs was a short life. Rudimentary conditions underground, overcrowded housing and malnutrition, meant sickness and disease took their tolls.

To us it is a wonder they chose such an existence. But for many this way of life was part of them.

William Jones observed the mining districts of Great Britain and wrote about Cornish miners in his publication, *The Treasure of the Earth*, in 1868:

> Working in such great depths of the earth, far removed from the cheerful influences of daylight, and surrounded with many dangers, would seem to most of us as a fearful occupation, but nature, kind mother of us all, gives us a measure of endurance to the human mind and frame, which circumstances strengthen, and habit makes endurable... It is a roving disposition that makes the sailor what he is; and as he too gets accustomed to his wild and perilous life, he passes carelessly through dangers that would appall a landman. So with the miner, he also has his excitement in the discovery of metallic veins underground, and in working his way into deeper recesses, intent on his labour, and without the distraction of changing objects that arrest the attention above ground.

Mining was in the blood, an almost integral part of their souls, and they could see no other way. They were simply content to be employed.

Each mine was managed by captains, who had the responsibility of overseeing all works. Grass captains managed surface work, while underground captains managed work below ground. Underground captains had in-depth practical knowledge of geology and could survey a mine for further mining exploitations.

It was the purser's job was to carry out all the book-keeping and wages and he would apportion the profits where they were due. Miners were divided into the self-employed, called tributers, and tut-workers, who were on a regular wage. However, it was the engineman, binders, pitman and head smith who were paid the most overall. Binders oversaw the maintenance of all timbers, the pitman the shafts and ladders.

Hundreds of mines were sunk in the nineteenth century. Wheal Mary Ann, Kit Hill Mines, Herodsfoot Mine, Wheal Kitty, Ding Dong and Cligga Head are some of the few names of renown. Most tin and copper mining was initially pursued along the North Coast from Cape Cornwall through St Just and Pendeen. Kenidjack Valley, Wheal Edward, Bottallack, Geevor and Levant Mines were never served by the mineral railway, but ores were transported by packhorse along the road to the docks at Penzance. Later, mines moved eastwards to Redruth, Camborne and Pool until they were spread throughout Cornwall in the 1860s.

Night and day the worked never ceased in these busy areas, with miners doggedly extracting the ores underground, unseen. For those who weren't mindful of the temperance movement, coming to the surface at the end of a shift would mean visiting one of the many 'winks'. Beer and spirits warmed the belly and made walking home, through all weathers, more bearable. Many miners, however, frowned on this practice as 'The Society for the Suppression of Drunkenness' had much influence in the reformation of the 'poor and vulgar' from about 1805.

To walk home, for many, in some of the wilder mining districts, would entail travelling several miles by foot across rough terrain. A narrow winding path, barely visible by the light of a lantern, or hole-pierced treacle tin, would make a way through exposed downs and across cairns. The sudden change of temperature from heat that would make a man's boots fill with sweat, to the pelting rain on winter nights was enough to slay some of the sicklier men.

The Beginnings

Long before the first engine house, in ancient times, the early settler discovered surface tin in hillsides and streambeds, exposed by wind and rain, such was the bounteous natural provision. The main ore of tin is cassiterite; a hard and unreactive mineral. The erosion of ground containing tin has, over time, produced tin-bearing gravels. These gravels produced the majority of tin found in streams running across hard granite towards the sea. Previous erosion by the elements caused the heavy tin ore to settle in places along the streambed. Running water constantly broke up the bed and tinners would dig up the heavier deposits.

An adaptation of this process was developed through time, and similar methods have been used throughout mining history. A channel of water would be diverted especially for the 'dressing process'. This entailed digging out the deposit, putting it into the dressing bed, and raking carefully and persistently against the flow of the water. Because of its high density a concentrate deposit of tin was formed and many impurities removed by the running water.

Once deep mining became widespread, much of the waste was deposited in rivers. A similar, but new type of streaming took place as workers re-treated the waste. The processing of tin ore has always involved the crushing and grinding of rock to separate out the highest grade of tin concentrate. The aim was to extract as much fine tin as possible. By the nineteenth century there were numerous processes and variations of washing alluvial deposits to recover tin oxide. The main principle remained consistent – gravity; tin being considerably heavier than the impurities attached to it. These waste products were burned, stamped and washed off. Terms such as buddling, chimming and tozing described these cleaning processes. In the 1890s the main dressing areas were found at Camborne and Redruth, although every mining district had skilled dressers.

Dumps from original mine workings were treated years later once dressing techniques improved and many profitable livings were had from old burrows that were picked over again.

'Tinners' have probably always been at work in the moors and cliffs of Cornwall, although the remains of their activities are difficult to precisely date. So much tinning has taken place over the centuries, that archeological remains show a range of different time periods. The continual turning of the soil and relentless flow of water has meant little conclusive evidence remains to identify where and how ancient man's tinning exploits began.

Romans came looking for metal, separating tin from gravel before mixing it with copper for bronze. Armour, helmets, shields, jewellery and goblets have all been excavated, dating back to these earliest times.

William Jones considers how brutal mining is, but compares conditions in 1868 with the past and finds them favourable:

> Among the ancients, to dig in mines was considered the most severe punishment for criminals. The persecuted Christians who escaped death were made to linger out a miserable existence in those dreadful places. They worked in water so stagnant that they frequently fell down dead.

Nowhere else in Europe was as rich in this natural resource as Cornwall. Explorers from afar risked the high seas for this most precious ore deposit.

Tin is a dark black-brown mineral and is more rare than other metals such as copper or iron. Tin streaming, being the simplest method of finding tin stone, has left many valleys showing signs of disturbed gravel beds – such as Fowey, Penpol, St Day, St Neot and Devoran. Tinners worked setts out on the open moors or along riverbanks using long-handled shovels and picks, searching for deposits. The St Austell area has many stream tinworks, as do the areas around St Erth and Hayle.

In the twelfth century the Charter of the Stanneries was declared. These were statutes outlining the lawful way to claim tin from the land. It was decreed that a tinner could look for tin, as was done since ancient times, on wasteland. The lord of the manor could demand a toll but otherwise had to leave the tinner undisturbed. For the first time in history the miner was his own master, independent, not a serf or hired labourer. The tax was levied only on the tin itself. The prospective tinner would make a claim on a plot and indicate its location by 'bounding' (sinking a pit and lining it with timber).

Once tin had been washed it was carried by packhorse or mule to the nearest blowing house for smelting. From here it had to be taken to the nearest coinage town, originally Truro, Helston, Lostwithiel or Liskeard. Here it was weighed, taxed and stamped with the Duchy arms.

Four times a year these coinage assemblies took place. They were great occasions for festivity. Several days would be spent taking pleasure from some of the profits. In several of the town's inns, or beside the stalls of market traders, hurling, drinking beer or cider, wrestling and cock fighting were some of the pastimes enjoyed by tinners.

As early as 1450, work began on underground tin excavation. These were the first 'open' surface workings – 'open' to the sky. At first it was carried out with the use of rope and rickety ladders; all the work done with hand tools.

Open pits called 'coffins' or 'goffins' were dug, sometimes only a few feet deep but at the most 50 feet, the waste being banked up alongside. Loose rubble was dug and thrown up out of the pit, shovel by shovel, or hoisted out of the trench by bucket and windlass for treatment. The race was always on against constant underground floodwater, filling the dark, dug holes faster than a man could work.

Primitive pumps were used to keep the water from hindering progress and shallow shafts sunk. The many lumps and bumps on today's landscape are telling signs of our predecessors digging for tin. Now all that remains are furrows and dips, the uneven ground and undulating landscape covered in heather and gorse.

Tin lodes could be seen on cliff outcrops and men began to chisel and chip away. The tinners were intent on retrieving vertical lodes and many of the early mines would have probably begun from these early cliff works along the North Coast. Considering the appalling winds and weather along this stretch of Atlantic coastline, and the jagged rock faces, these hardy men must have been frequently injured as they daily diced with death.

Often wet and cold, it would be slippery underfoot, and an ever-present threat of falling debris overhead put lives at risk. It must have been extraordinarily difficult and a hugely demanding task to tunnel into the hard rock with basic implements. A reckless and daring man would be needed to work at these heights in such arduous conditions day after day.

It was exacting work requiring precise cutting skills to excavate the hard rock face, without the advantage of mechanised machinery. Quarrying techniques were perfected through time, using essential hand tools such as crowbars, picks, mallets, axes and shovels.

If a stubborn piece refused to budge, they would light a furze fire underneath; the heat and sudden cooling, after water was sloshed on, would cause the rock to fracture and crack. Ingenuity won the day.

It wasn't until the 1700s that gunpowder was generally used to blast open the rock. This dangerous practice was widely used, but feared, because appalling accidents from premature or misfired explosions killed men outright.

It was the Cornishman William Bickford who invented the safety fuse, giving miners those much-needed extra seconds to move to safety before the blast. Using gunpowder became less hazardous as a consequence, but there were still thick and unhealthy fumes following each firing, which made working conditions almost unbearable.

From the original coffin workings, new underground mining methods developed. Tunnels were driven into the lode to expose the ore at greater depths. During the 1600s adits were used to drain the water away, as well as to water-wheels and horse-driven pumps.

Shafts had been used for some time and were essential for ventilation purposes. Shafts began to be sunk below the natural drainage level as mines grew deeper. Mine shafts came in a range of shapes and sizes and were the essential link to the underground world of a mine. Early shafts often had a specific purpose, such as pumping or hoisting and could be built at an angle to follow a steep lode. However, more recent shafts were large, multi-purpose, vertical and deep.

The main and most taxing difficulty faced in deep mining has always been the removal of water. Besides teams of horses, every possible system of mechanised water-wheel, windlass and bucket were tried.

Pumps worked by a simple water-wheel were effective only to a point, so enormous progress was made when steam-power pumping was developed in the eighteenth century. This process enabled ever-increasing deep-shaft

mining. Thomas Newcomen's newly invented steam engine was first introduced at Wheal Vor, near Helston, in 1715. These original designs for steam
engines were adapted from hand and windmill pumps.

But it was Richard Trevithick, a Camborne man, who is most famous for
having invented the high-pressure steam engine in 1811. Cornish beam
engines were predominantly used for pumping water up from the deep mine,
but were also used for ore crushing (powering stamps) and for hoisting up
and down the shaft.

Before dependable steel wire ropes were adopted for winding up and
down the shafts, chains were used. In more recent times large electronic
hoists were installed.

A beam engine is essentially a steam engine with a vertical piston that
pushes or pulls one end of a massive beam. With a central pivot, the other
end of the beam has a pump or other mechanical device. The beam was cast
from iron and could weigh more than 50 tons. The outer end of the beam pro-
jected over the pump shaft and was connected to the pump rod, passing
down the shaft.

With the closure of Cornish mines many of these magnificent beam
engines were broken for scrap. The depression in the tin industry coincided
with the expansion of the china clay industry, so a number of mine engines
were relocated to the St Austell area to operate pumps there.

A Cornish deep-shaft mine is a bewildering maze of tunnels and shafts
at various levels. Tunnels were worked along a lode, which was rich in tin.
Steps and shafts gave access to each level and there may have been a
series of lodes running parallel with each other. Distances between levels
varied from mine to mine. Some mines would eventually sink 2,000 to
3,000 feet below the surface with tunnels extending several miles under
the sea bed.

In Victorian times the men would work at putting on stoping timber
staging, which was attached to the side of the tunnel and could stand several
metres high. They used hammers and hand drills in the 1900s to extract the
ore by the light of candles. Sometimes a plank would be placed precariously
across open shafts enabling men to carry equipment across.

The start of the nineteenth century was the greatest era of Cornish
copper and tin mining. With the major problem of drainage solved by high-
pressure beam engines there was an increase in the output of ore.

Thousands of packhorses and mules were used along dirt tracks to
transport ore and coal by packsaddle to and from local ports. Carrying
mules were introduced in Cornwall during the seventeenth century.

*The incline at Portreath, enabling ore and coal to be transported
to and from the sailing vessels bound for Wales.*

Before this, dogs were apparently used to carry across crags and difficult terrain. It was entirely upon the sturdy backs of horses that the whole of Cornwall's merchandise was transported. Very occasionally carts were used, but in mining districts the roads were notoriously difficult to negotiate. Sledges were employed for heavier equipment and tram rods were laid down in 1791. Horses were then used to pull trams carrying ore and supplies between mines.

Geevor Tin Mine

Nobody knows the precise time that mining came to the district of St Just on the extreme west of Cornwall's peninsula. It seems likely that there has always been exploitation of these tin and copper lodes dating back to pre-history. There are signs of outcrop workings, streamworks, adits and water-powered dressing floors along the Atlantic coast believed to date back to medieval times.

Now the mine burrows are covered in bracken, and evidence of industrial workings are scattered through the fields around St Just. From Morvah to the Nanjulian Valley, this stretch of moorland by the sea includes a group of mines, two of which were among the most productive in Cornwall, and Geevor was the last Cornish mine to close.

An almost unbroken chain of mines stretches along the coast from the

Cape of Cornwall to Zennor, St Ives and Lelant. St Just United Mine was established in 1869 and larger mines, such as Bottallack and Levant Mines, were incorporated into Geevor. Levant was one of the great tin and copper mines of Cornwall.

Mining has shaped the landscape around this area and signs of mining are rarely out of sight. Engine houses in ruin, remains of smithies, dressing floors, count houses and the head gear of Geevor Mine are an integral and familiar part of the skyline.

Lodes have been worked scarring the fields and coastline. Some areas are riddled with small shafts and the surface of the ground will always be unstable.

From small beginnings many mines joined together to form larger mines in the eighteenth century until North Levant Mine became a major mine by the nineteenth century. Most of Cornwall's tin and copper mining was carried out along this North Coast stretch at this time.

Geevor Tin Mine on the cliffs around Pendeen eventually closed in 1990. The tin market crash of 1986 caused nearly 300 men to lose their jobs and although pumps remained operational, recovery was never possible. When the pumps were finally turned off, this ended nearly 300 years of virtually continuous mining on the site.

Geevor was originally part of the copper mining district but workings were developed for tin in 1840 in East Levant Mine. It was in 1911 that the now famous company known as Geevor Tin Mines Ltd was formed. Despite a few brief closures, Geevor had survived two world wars and carried on mining despite the shortage of skilled miners. Throughout the 1960s and 1970s exploration took place to locate new ore and the future looked encouraging as tin prices rose.

It was devastating for the local area when world tin prices collapsed and the mine closed, causing economic hardship for many. There did seem to be a revival of hope in 1988 when the mine was temporarily brought back into service but a decision was eventually made to finally stop the pumps.

In 1993 Geevor was opened as a museum and heritage site. Many of the buildings and much of the machinery show the development of mining throughout the century. Geevor is dramatically set on the cliffs of Pendeen, close to the lighthouse, and was originally called Wheal an Giver, meaning ground occupied by goats. What makes it unique is that the site retains a working appearance and is not in ruins like so many of its neighbours. Even though Geevor will never be a working mine again, it provides an admirable representation of the Cornish mining industry.

The Tinner's Home

A tinner's household and community, even though verging on poverty, was nevertheless close to a consistent, albeit meager, living. In Victorian times throughout Britain, prospects in other industrial areas weren't much better. At least mining families could live in relatively healthy surroundings, not like the slums of inner cities.

The mine was the centre of a community, a focus for men, women and children, who were all employed in some capacity. By all accounts there was a sense of belonging and camaraderie, people helping each other out through each successive shift of day or night. Living close by one another, the daily struggles of working family life were shared with neighbours and friends.

However, there was an element within the mining community that caused offence to William Jones's considered sense of seemliness:

> I have given the bright side of the Cornish miners' general character, but there are exceptions and, unfortunately, these are numerous. Many are the improvident habits, the prevailing evil of this class of men. Eating and drinking bouts, called 'choruses' are all too frequent, especially on Saturday.

Many of the streets of St Just developed around the mining industry and The Cape's landscape has clusters of buildings built by the mining generation

In the early 1800s many would build their own small cob cottage. Although solid in structure, they were susceptible to the notorious Cornish damp sea mists, driving storms and drizzle. A furze fire and the warmth of many occupants would barely help to drive out the damp rising from the earth, lime ash or flag floor. In addition, the landowner could legally take back the building and land after three generations.

For the great numbers of miners settling in the region later in the century, towns were built. Row upon row of back-to-back terraced houses, two up two down, a yard and laundry room outside, and a high-strung washing line to catch the Atlantic winds, sprang up. These uniform façades remain in many towns such as Redruth, Pool, Camborne, St Just and Pendeen. Granite built and enduring, these cottages have remained through the rise and fall of many a man's dreams and aspirations. They have stood witness to the once flourishing, then derelict, then flourishing again, then final demise of an industrial mining era.

Jones described what he saw in Cornwall:

> If you go into a mining district in Cornwall you will see, not far from the mine works, rows of neat little cottages, many of them built

This row of cottages in Queen Street, in St Just, typifies the old mining cottages.

by the miners themselves after the work of the mine is done, most of them are extremely clean in the interior, and here you many find them seated at comfortable fires, frequently reading – for most of them are intelligent and thoughtful men, or in the summer evenings they work in their little gardens or in the potato fields, many of the cottages having a piece of ground for cultivation attached to them. Frequently to become experienced floriculturists and at some of the flower shows that occur annually in several of the towns they often carry off the prizes. What a relief such pleasing pursuits must be to men employed for several hours in the day in the bowels of the earth, far removed from light and from wholesome air.

Miners' cottages were known to be well ordered in general. Daily routines of shift work would mean several generations could work at different times of the day. Two centuries ago Cornwall's population was surprisingly greater in number than today, despite significantly less housing stock. Overcrowding was common in rural districts. A family including several adult children could share restricted sleeping quarters. This was made more bearable if some worked the night shift, returning to the warm sheets of those who had just left for the day shift. So the beds were barely empty. Jones writes:

> Some miners also are expert carpenters and make their own furni-
> ture, and those near the coast employ some of their leisure time in
> fishing. They are generally brave and courageous men, rendered so,
> in a great measure, by the nature of their employment.

The miner would go to work typically wearing a jacket over shirt and trousers, boots without socks and a bowler hat, which was stiffened by painting it with resin. On this there would be a clay holder for a candle; up to six spare candles would be needed for a shift underground. A tool kit containing drills, shovels, picks, sledgehammer and wedges would need to be carried up and down the ladders daily.

Women worked in tin streams, but were prevented, along with children under the age of ten, from working underground by the 1842 Mines and Collieries Act. Once brought to the surface, tin ores needed to be broken by hand. This was carried out by mechanical stone-breakers at the end of the nineteenth century, but prior to this by women (bal-maidens).

Workers would hand pick and sort the waste on the surface of the mine. Waste lumps were broken off the ore with a hammer and then 'cobbed' by women. The cobbing broke off all the fine pieces of waste from around the ore. This was then crushed again by the bal-maidens, who used large flat hammers upon iron slabs.

As well as her own shift, the woman still strove to make a meal for the family with the few resources she had at her disposal. Salted fish, potatoes, barley bread and tea were sometimes varied with an egg or scrap of home-cured bacon.

A tinner's broth rarely consisted of butcher's meat. Mutton or beef were substituted with vegetables and accompanied by a 'mossel' of barley bread. Wheaten bread at twice the price was savoured only on feast days.

The hungry 1840s saw many famished and feeble men barely able to make it to and from their shift. Food was prohibitively expensive and, unlike in some rural areas, had to be paid for instead of grown. Turnips, generally used as cattle fodder, kept many working-class families free from the debilitating effects of malnutrition.

Water was also scarce in some districts as wells were drained dry by the mines. Families sometimes had to walk several miles for essential supplies, relying on a nearby parish's stream.

On the upside, laundering was made much easier as warm water from the engine house could serve a community of women on washday. They would traipse across the downs, carrying laundry trays and bags to the mine house, only to return to their small cottage with little room for drying, and barely enough space for making up a furze fire.

Early marriages and many children were the norm in Cornwall, and desertion of the marital home was a rare thing. Sanitary conditions were squalid in places, St Just and Lelant especially, so infant and child mortality was high.

Mineral Tramways
Cornwall's very first railways were horse- or man-powered, not driven by steam locomotive as we might imagine. The packhorse was limited in how much it could carry. The weight and enormity of sacks of goods meant using pack animals down earthen tracks was laborious. But with a wagon helped along by a rail, the animal could pull greater amounts more efficiently. The earliest rail links to Portreath Harbour were made of timber in the 1600s and served foundries, mines and potteries.

In the eighteenth century cast-iron rails were introduced, but because of their brittle nature, work was often hindered by breakage. Plate was used for a time but it was wrought-iron rails that eventually solved the problem.

By using horse-drawn wagons it was possible to transport greater weights of ore from the mine to sailing vessels that would take it to the smelters in Wales. On the return journey to the mine, the wagons would be loaded up with coal, brought back from Welsh mines and used in ever-increasing amounts in Cornwall's steam pump engines.

Another tram road was opened in 1819 and served the mines at Wheal Buller and Lanner Hill near the village of Carnkie, taking tin to Devoran and the Fal estuary. Like the Portreath line, the Redruth and Chasewater line was horse drawn.

However, in 1837 the first steam locomotive hauled a cargo of coal from Hayle to Carn Brea. This was the start of the transportation of commercial goods by steam and led to the development of a passenger line in Cornwall. It was the mineral railway, though, that rendered the faithful packhorse obsolete. The horse and wagon plodding along a stretch of rail could not compete with the speed of steam even if it was only up to speeds of 30 miles per hour.

Month by month the thousands of tram horses, mules and their drivers went into permanent retirement and only a few of these noble creatures were left to be used on the yards around the mines.

Declining Years

Cornish mining enjoyed the heights of prosperity during the 1850s and 1860s. There were more than 173 copper mines in production at Fowey Consols, Tresavean, Gwennap Consols, Wheal Basset, Wheal Buller and United Mines. The mining industry at this time was looking to copper rather than tin as its economic mainstay. The Duchy's entire economy was based predominantly on mining and its ancillary trades.

However, foreign mines began increasingly to threaten Cornwall's domination of the world market. Copper was discovered in Lake Superior in the United States, Spanish Peninsula mines became more productive and Chile and Australia were beginning to occupy a far stronger position.

The great collapse came between the years of 1865 and 1870. Cornwall lost its monopoly on the world's copper trade and production plummeted in response to falling copper prices. Even the mines that struggled on in the hope of recovery began to lose their most skilled miners. The outlook became dismal and as the slump grew worse thousands of miners emigrated.

Tin mining could not sustain the great numbers of workers. St Day lost six mines in as many years with more than 3,000 jobs gone. Families left their homes for better prospects overseas leaving street upon street of abandoned, empty cottages.

Some copper mines were able to extend exploration to lodes on deeper

The Phoenix United Mines, Liskeard, 1908.

levels then transfer to tin. Those that passed from copper to tin production included Wheal Kitty, Carn Brea, South Crofty, Bottallack, and mines around St Agnes and St Just.

Even so, a great many mines were closed down and abandoned. A steady stream of skilled Cornish miners departed these shores for the mines of North and South America, Australia, South Africa and New Zealand. Many left their extended families behind, sending money back home to loved ones in Cornwall. Others emigrated with their family members. Those who remained continued to find some work in remaining tin mines, quarries and foundries.

As mining developed to its peak in the early 1800s, related industries grew as a consequence. Harvey & Co.'s Foundry, and the Copperhouse Foundry at Hayle fabricated mining equipment. Cornish beam engines were dispatched all over the world and Hayle was renowned as a centre of excellence.

Cornish tin mining continued throughout the twentieth century with the introduction of electricity, compressed air drills, fast-moving hoists and high explosives. But Cornish mining would never be the same again.

Any revival of mining in Cornwall is now considered unlikely; it has ended for all time. Mile upon mile of water-filled underground shafts, lodes and tunnels, once fervently disgorged, lie abandoned.

Isolated and bare, the granite engine houses stand steadfast as formidable memorials to a now nonfunctioning tin-mining industry. Abandoned, weather has worn away the stonework, opportunists have helped themselves to some of the slates, and once-sturdy timbers have rotted. After decades of neglect many are just clustered mounds of rubble starting to become overrun with vegetation. Once they would have rung out the constant chug of the massive steam-driven engine, now all that is left is an eerie silent reminder of a once-productive past. Yet they also represent life, thousands of lives.

CHAPTER 4

FISHING

In the past if a Cornishman was not mining underground, streaming for tin or working the soil for a living he would likely be gaining his livelihood from fishing. Home would have been in one of the numerous clusters of villages hugging the sea's edge and his boat would be close by in the harbour. The harbour formed the heart of many Cornish fishing towns and villages. With cottages nestled in rows up the surrounding hillsides, behind the harbour walls, these clustered communities once clung to an existence that was reliant on the tides.

Marine technology has changed the Cornish fishing industry beyond all recognition. The classic sailing luggers have been replaced by motor-powered vessels, which have highly sophisticated sonar equipment on board that is able to locate shoals of fish with ease. Because these sensors are so efficient, modern fishing methods have seriously depleted the oceans' fish stocks. Without careful conservation and restraint there is a very strong likelihood that the fishing industry may become obsolete in some coastal towns.

With the passing of so many traditional methods, it is hard to envisage the Cornish harbours of yesteryear crowded with brown-sailed luggers or even steam-powered boats. Every fisherman was an expert in his own seabed territory, adept at catching his specialty of edible fish, falling into one of two categories: those whose habitat is deep on the sea bed (demersal) and those living closer to the surface (prelagic). To catch those deep on the bed a series of hooks on lines were used. Surface fish were caught in the meshes of nets lurking up to several fathoms down.

A fisherman's main concern was to keep watch on the weather and avoid misadventure, ensuring he and his companions were kept safe onboard. Danger preyed on his boat so he needed to take every precaution. Ever watch-ful of changes in the wind or tide he knew the slightest misjudgment of timing could mean imminent danger and possible disaster for his crew. It was a battle against the weather, and risks were a constant part of the fisherman's lot.

This charming postcard painting of St Ives in 1912 recreates the
timeless activity of selling herrings on the harbourside.

Despite perhaps having a cautious attitude in theory, the gamble, the result of
which needed to actually bring home a full catch, often overrode prudence.

Even though the Cornish coast is known for its rough seas and tempera-
mental tidal changes, in many ways the fisherman's life was less hazardous than
that of the tinner. A tinner gambled on each new prospect, never sure if the supply of tin would provide enough to survive. The fisherman wasn't challenged in
this way. In former times there was an ever-bountiful supply of fish, it was just
a matter of locating them when the tides and weather were favourable.

Take a walk through seaside towns such as St Ives today and there are
crowds of visitors intent on perusing the endless arrays of knick-knacks. Every
conceivable type of enterprise has been set up to ply for the trade of passing
tourists: pasty shops, ice-cream parlours, shell shops and surf retailers, all
bursting out on to the tiny winding streets with their wares. Art
galleries with seascape prints and paintings, creative crafts and handmade
jewellery are accommodated in buildings that were once the homes of
fishermen and their families.

There is little left today to hint at what St Ives once was. This delightful
town, with quaint, cobbled, meandering pavements, haphazard roof lines and
the tiniest of cottages is now a holiday destination for those seeking a seaside
escape. The rows of tiny dwellings are spruced up with immaculate paintwork,

This posed image from 1907 is evocative of a century earlier.
The tableau illustrates a time when fishermen were reliant on sail.

pretty arrangements of bedding plants and contrived interiors all aimed at creating a tourist's idyll. But years ago these streets would have been rank with the smell of curing fish.

St Ives was the main pilchard-fishing centre of Cornwall with annual catches that once exceeded the whole of the rest of the Duchy combined. Nearly the whole community was involved in the fishing industry in some way or another. Many backyards and cellars were given over to the packing process, with salt-encrusted walls and floors running with the dregs of fish oil. You would have needed a particular purpose to come to St Ives back then, such was the rancid smell of processing fish. The gutters and drains would be buzzing with flies and gulls would be scrapping overhead as the fish swill and waste made its way down the gullies towards the quay.

There were all sorts of cottage industries associated with the fishery. A great many people were employed making ropes and netting, repairing boats and sloops, with canvas covers being sewn and oiled ready for inclement weather. The wooden casks for pilchard transportation were handmade by hundreds of local craftsmen, timber being imported from overseas. If a skipper required a new boat he would enlist the services of local boat builders. Everything was made by hand locally, using timber sawn in a saw-pit and ironwork from the local foundry.

Before synthetic fibres were invented in the twentieth century, nets were made from cotton and hemp. To prevent these natural fibres rotting it was necessary to soak them in preservative. A solution derived from oak bark boiled in water for many hours was used. Nets would be mended, soaked in the preservative (cutched) and laid out to dry.

The fishing industry had its heyday between the mid-eighteenth and mid-nineteenth centuries when pilchards were the most prized catch. The pilchard (*Clupea pilchardus*) resembles a herring but is distinguishable by being shorter, rounder and fatter, yet larger than a sardine. These fish frequented the coasts of Cornwall and the south-west of Ireland, migrating from the Atlantic around the Isles of Scilly into Cornish waters from July onwards. The main season was traditionally between harvest and All Saints' Day (1 November), although fishermen could be confident that they would remain along the Cornish coast throughout November and into December.

After spawning in the spring, pilchards would make their way from the entrance of the English Channel towards land. Pilchards were actually a subtropical fish. They were a larger, older, more mature sardine than those caught in the Mediterranean. Shoals came closer to the shore in late summer when the entire fishing community would become involved in their processing. Every man, woman and child would wait in anticipation of the shoals arriving in the daytime and be prepared to work consistently through the season until the annual 'harvest from the sea' was all brought in.

The Cornish had been catching and eating pilchards since earliest times. They were consumed fresh in the summer or salted and cured in the winter months. This fish was the Cornish staple diet. The pilchard fishery was always a part of life stretching back into early Cornish history. As a national export industry it precipitated legislation in Parliament and its fluctuations in international trade caused much interest in the business elite of each successive decade. Each season's success was watched over with vigilance as every fishing village from Plymouth to Land's End had pilchard fleets costing thousands of pounds of investment and capital.

Hevva!

It was the huer's cry of 'Hevva! Hevva!' through his trumpet that heralded the beginnings of a pilchard-shoal catch. It was the huer's task to alert all the villagers of a shoal's arrival in the bay. From an outpost high on the cliffs, he intently scanned the waters for a telltale sign of the pilchards' arrival. Sometimes he would be seen sitting on a bench outdoors, while in other places a cottage was provided where he could eat a meal and warm himself by a fire. Cottages frequented by watchmen along the coast were known as lookout points, where they acquainted themselves with the activities of wildlife in the sea below.

From the huer's vantage point he could direct the fishing vessels towards the shoal with a series of hand signals. Each motion was understood perfectly well by those below. He would be armed with two furze bushes, covered in a white calico cloth, which he would use to signal to the fishermen, who bided their time in boats down in the harbour. These fishermen

This huer's hut has been preserved as a tourist site on the cliffs of Newquay. It is typical of the kind of building that was used by the huer waiting for the sighting of a catch. Note that the stairs lead to the roof, where he could have stood to wave his instructions to the boats in the bay below. This photograph was taken in 1958 long after the building was vacated.

would wait under the cover of a tarpaulin to keep out the worst of any rain, or shelter from the sun, and spent their days smoking and mending nets, waiting until their fishing skills were required.

The seine, which consisted of three boats and two nets, represented a team of at least ten fishermen. The seine fishermen were the wealthiest of the fishermen and they generally worked for partnerships. Two men would own three boats, two nets and storage and curing premises on shore. They would pay weekly wages for the crew, huer and processors, reinvesting profits into boat and net repairs.

After months of being moored on dry ground in the parching sun these boats were taken down to the harbour just before the season began. It was generally known that pilchards were on their way from passing ships that traversed the fishing stations on other business. Teams of men were needed to lug the heavy vessels, then a coordinated 'Ho, launch a bo!' was shouted out as they worked together dragging them across the golden sand to the sea one by one. Once in the water all the necessary kit was brought out of storage from the seine lofts. Oars, anchor, seine net, coiled up ready and mended over the winter, were all put onboard in preparation.

Each morning the crew would check the tide and weather and if conditions were favourable the craft would be rowed out and an anchor put down in wait for a shoal. The whole village was on call, carrying on with daily tasks but always half listening for a shout of 'Hevva!' to ring out.

The boats could be at anchor for several consecutive days in preparation for a catch. The first of the seine's three boats was a kind of galley, being broad, low and sharp. A typical size would have been about 33 feet keel and 12 feet beam. Six men were needed to row the first boat because it had no sails. The main 'steerer' boat carried the principal net, about 440 yards in length, which was called a seine. The second boat was of the same size but was called the follower and this held the second net called a tuck seine, which was smaller at 160 yards in length and up to 36 yards in depth. This net was cast inside the other and was the one the men worked from in lifting out the catch, transferring the fish onto the decks and then into the baskets. This boat required the same sized crew as the steerer.

The third and smallest boat was a lurker, so called as it watched for the appearance of fish, carrying out a similar job to the huer on the cliffs. The few men onboard scanned the ocean, led by the 'capstun', guiding the other vessels to ensure the shoal was captured in full.

The pilchards would appear as a red, purple and silver stain in the ocean. Overhead flocks of seagulls and diving gannets were a sure sign of the shoal's location. Whales, porpoises and dolphins holding a feeding frenzy around the shoal was also a sure indication it had arrived close to land. The jubilant sound of villagers alerted everyone concerned that the pilchards were making their way in their millions towards them. Shouts of 'Hevo! Heva!' echoed through the streets as men rushed down to their boats and women and children crowded around in lively anticipation. Everyone was anxious that this catch should be a success and the next year's income sustained.

The urgency of responding to the huer's instructions meant all the fishermen acted with swift dexterity and responded in unison to the huer's frantic arm movements. It was a mad rush as they all rowed and the crew from the lurker shouted instructions. The crowds were gathered on the quay and the children would cheer the men on, knowing full well the importance of the task ahead. The boats would be launched in rapid succession. The hope was to catch an entire shoal. Once the seine net had encircled the majority of the shoal the second net would be attached to the first and the process of bringing the catch closer to the surface began. A successful catch meant food in their bellies and money to spare for the winter ahead. There were hundreds if not thousands of people involved in a day's work, each one active and part of the communal process.

Shooting the Seine
From a seemingly relaxed pace carrying out everyday tasks, the fishing village would burst into frenetic activity. Tuckers, carters and curers would all work together with one purpose. Tuckers would gather together their baskets and buckets making their way to shore, ready to collect fish from the boats. Carters would tack up their horse and cart or put bridle and packsaddle on a mule so they could transport the pilchards to the fish cellars. The curers would make their way to the quay or open up the cellars checking that the salt was ready. Everyone was prepared to help out where necessary, all aware that time was of the essence to ensure that the catch remained fresh and intact.

The operation of shooting the seine net into the water was a marvel to watch. The need for precision and the co-ordination of all the crew meant the process was carried out as a synchronised and succinct operation. There was a sense of excitement as all the men, endeavouring to work swiftly, prevented the shoal escaping.

At the moment the tuck seine produced its burden above the water the sight was evidently beautiful beyond description. Leaping and playing together the blue and silver reflections of the fish were a blaze of splendour. From a distance the glistening array looked like a mass of diamonds as their silver scales caught the light.

This is when the process of warping took place. The immense circular net carrying its valuable catch was warped into five to seven fathoms of water. The shoal was alive and bubbling in the tucking net as the fishermen strove to contain it. The two ends of the tuck were gathered together and the assembled boats and barges started to carry the shoal ashore portion by portion. This process of tucking took place all day until the whole shoal was taken up with the fleet of boats waiting close by until it was their turn to receive a deck load of pilchards. Every available basket and bucket was used to carry the frantic fish to shore.

If it wasn't possible to finish in one day, the seine net could remain in place for several days as tides and weather allowed. Sometimes a shoal was so huge it took several days to tuck, there being insufficient labour to process such a great catch. The pilchards remained entrapped for the duration of the tucking time. Every effort was made to keep the shoals alive inside the seine and only an amount that could be managed in the day was removed.

The greatest problem with any fish was keeping it fresh. Local markets could sell a proportion of the catch but the poor roads and reliance on

Here is a typical scene in Newlyn in 1908, which was witnessed in every fishing harbour in Cornwall for centuries. Horses and carts, packsaddled mules and the labour-intensive rowing and sailing boats were commonplace and essential to landing a catch.

horse-drawn transport meant it was not possible to send fish to distant parts. Some local people arrived with wicker baskets on their backs with a leather strap supported from the forehead. They would then take small portions of the catch to sell in nearby villages and farmsteads.

Waiting on the quay, and on the beach, were horse and carts, pack mules and women from the salting houses. Theirs was the task of transporting the catch ready for the salting process. Smoking pilchards in smoke houses, pickling them in tanks of salt water, and dry salting them were some of the experimental methods tried, but these were less successful than bulking. The bulking method that was eventually used by most curing cellars relied on great quantities of salt. Although some of it was home-produced sea salt, the rest came from other counties such as Devon, but the majority was shipped in from France. A much larger number of people was required to land and then prepare the fish for curing than was needed to catch them. When the pilchards were first brought ashore they were placed in a gurry, a square, wooden, open box with handles at each end. Each one was carried by two strong carriers and could hold up to 1,000 fish.

The fish cellars, now redundant throughout Cornwall, were used to prepare pilchards for preservation. Fish were packed in layers, sprinkled with salt and then pressed using heavy stones to squeeze out the blood and oil. They were then packed in this preserved state for export.

There was no need to gut or fillet the fish as they only have tiny innards, with contents that are almost imperceptible they are so minute. Pilchards were considered to be merchantable at about eight to ten inches in length, but frequently smaller ones were mixed in as well. These smaller fish had a thinner coat of scales that broke apart during processing so were thrown aside and used on the land as a natural fertilizer.

The cellar usually consisted of a large stone rectangular building, often with a courtyard and net lofts overhead. It took two men to carry a gurry of fish to the cellar where they were unloaded onto a specially designed floor. Pebbles were implanted at intervals into the hardened base and gutters sloped towards a central pit, which was lined with a cast ready to receive the dregs of oil and blood. The oil that seeped out through gaps in the cobbled floor was retained and used for industrial machines. Farmers used the salt, water and offal as manure to replenish the soil.

Women mostly carried out this curing work and their children would help. All women aged between 16 and 60 worked together, squabbling and jesting, shrieking for 'more salt' or 'more fish', the children scuffling up and down with buckets as fast as they could. The fish would be piled on the floor and layered in mounds up to five feet high with salt. It was vitally important to ensure that the pilchards arrived in the cellars absolutely fresh. The ideal method ensured that the fish would all be processed and laid in salt without exposing them unsalted to the air. It was essential to get them in the cellars and imbibing the salt within the first few hours of the catch coming onshore.

The fish would remain 'in bulk' on the floor for up to six weeks. The majority of the salt dissolved into a 'pickle', which then drained through the bulk and ran off at the bottom. This occurred in the first few days of the curing process. The fish were then taken out of the bulk in which they were originally laid, sifted and ordered, separated from the salt, although some salt would be retained due to the fish's natural oily, absorbent quality. They would then be thoroughly washed clean, and packed in dry or loose casks pressed very close. These casks were specifically designed to allow leakage and were called hogsheads. Rather like a straight-sided barrel, they had tiny joints that allowed the fish to be pressed under large pressing stones. Up to 3,000 fish would be carefully arranged in a circular pattern in layers, and the hogshead was then sealed. Considerable pressure from great granite boulders with a system of levers was applied and the oil would seep out from the crevices in the cask, which would be retained for burning in lamps. Pressing took up to three weeks. The strong pressure meant that air was not free to pass between the fish so they were therefore fit to be transported abroad without danger of decay. Canning in oil didn't begin until the mid-1870s when the first factories were opened in Mevagissey and Newlyn.

There was always enough fish to feed all the households in the vicinity. Every larder locally had a store of salted pilchards for the year ahead. Domestically, pilchards were packed tight into an earthenware jar called a bussa, pickled in brine and kept for the winter. Those that weren't used to supply the neighbourhood were washed and packed into hogsheads, bought by merchants, and transported to the nearest ports for export. Italy, Portugal and Spain were the main recipients. The Roman Catholic faith with its precepts that required abstinence from meat on certain days was an incidental boost to the pilchard fishery. It was said to be because of Catholics' observance of Lent and eating fish on Fridays that pilchards were required in such numbers.

The most important years for the pilchard fishery were in the early 1800s. At that time there were seines along the Lizard, St Mawes, Coverack, Cadgwith, Portloe, Looe, Fowey, Polkerris and Mevagissey. The market house in Penzance, built in 1615, was a focal point for many merchants coming down from Falmouth and Penryn. Transporting boats came from London to collect the hogsheads of cured pilchards. However, the harbours of St Ives, Looe and Padstow were just as active in trade. Songs were made up to celebrate the catch and the end of the season, and they were sung in the inns as the fishermen reflected with gladness on their successes.

St Ives' long history of processing pilchards was dramatically brought to a close. The stocks of fish that were cured and exported in abundance up until the late 1880s suddenly diminished. The pilchard deserted these Cornish shores and the exact reason remains a mystery, although over fishing is a likely cause. In 1869 there were 286 seine companies registered in St Ives, but by 1900 only 30 remained. Changing tastes abroad also meant that the Cornish pilchard was less desirable after the nineteenth century. Hundreds of years of activity in the numerous fish cellars and quays laden with piles of fish became mere memories.

One can only imagine the desperation of the families who had relied so heavily on the seine fishing for their survival. Merchants were aware of where the shoals frequented so many single fishermen's skills were sought on foreign shores. But for those left behind, it was ingenuity and adapting to fishing using other methods that enabled them to beat poverty.

There were a few notable seines still cast out, but the fish had gone and consequently the huers and seiners went too. The mass summer invasions ceased and boats waited in vain. Sadly for the fishing communities, the last great memorable catch was made in St Ives in 1907.

By the early twentieth century all the buildings used for pilchard processing had been converted into stores and the seine nets tied up and left to rot. Seining will never take place again; it belongs to an era when fishermen sat passively and waited for a shoal. Now they go off searching for fish using every electronic and mechanical devise available to help them. One by one the boats were broken up, the fish cellars were converted and a centuries-old industry with its numerous practices and skills disappeared.

Drifters

By the 1870s it became apparent that the pilchard industry was in decline. Pilchards were also caught in drift nets further away from the shore along with other seasonal fish such as mackerel. Fishermen, who were called drovers or drivers, used drift nets. A net of 700 or 800 feet in length was put out to sea off the stern of the boat. Corks ran along the top and the bottom was weighed down with pieces of lead so the net hung like a massive wall in the sea. The pilchards would then become caught up and their entrapped bodies would need to be retrieved as the net was hauled in. This kind of fishing was best carried out at night or on cloudy days so that the fish were unable to see the fishermen's activities in the murky waters. Herrings were caught specifically using such drift-net methods. On close inspection the herring and mackerel are very different. By comparing the turn of their bodies, the size of their eyes and scales and the insertion of the pectoral fins it is possible to discern both the similarities and differences. The pilchard is much thicker, rounder and fatter.

The seine fishermen, however, blamed the drift fishing boats for the lack of pilchards closer to land. There was much controversy surrounding drift fishermen's activities as the techniques they used were said to discourage the shoals of pilchards, breaking them up and scattering them. The many miles of drift nets meant that the shoals were dispersed and prevented from entering the bays in such masses.

The boats used to lay drift nets were called luggers, having masts fore and aft. The hulls were traditionally painted with hot tar each year, sealing the seams with pitch and killing off any marine life on the timbers. The St Ives lugger's mast position differed from that of other areas such as Mount's Bay, and east Cornwall designs varied again.

The stretch of coast east of the Fal sustained fishing from St Mawes to Portholland including Portscatho and Portloe. The towns of Mevagissey,

The fish market at Looe in 1936.

Gorran, Polperro and Looe were thriving fishing ports and fed supplies to Plymouth and beyond.

St Ives harbour, with its sweeping bay leading to the Hayle estuary, dries out at low tide. This fishing town dominated the fishing along the North Coast, the only rival being Padstow. Other harbours such as Boscastle, Port Isaac and Newquay were tiny villages and therefore posed little competition. Mount's Bay, between Land's End and the Lizard Point, was premium fishing ground with the main ports being at Newlyn and the smaller town of Mousehole. Porthleven had a fleet of fishing luggers kept in the harbour and every cove west of the Lizard point was a fishing village, Coverack, Mullion, Porthoustock, Cadgwith and Porthallow and up as far as the Helford Passage and the Fal estuary.

A fishing boat was designed to suit local needs and its structure and shape varied from port to port. St Ives boats were built taking account of the short-breaking seas in the bay and were shallow underneath (shallow draft) so they sat easily on the sandy harbour bed at low tide. Larger boats were used for drifting after mackerel off shore from March to June. Then these larger vessels would go right out into the Atlantic following herrings. The inshore fishermen kept to local waters in their little boats but those in search of herring would venture as far as Ireland and Scotland.

There were always conflicts of interest between the drifters and the seiners, although the seiners were protected by a series of biased acts of Parliament. Arguments arose as restrictions prevented inshore drift fishing during the pilchard season, but as seining declined in the 1870s resentment among the drifters increased. They openly flouted the laws and were penalised greatly for 'poaching': sometimes the drifter's nets were confiscated, causing open hostility between the two branches of fishery. Many arguments ensued involving extended families, through several generations, resulting in the magistrate's intervention to resolve savage disputes. A range of measures intended to regulate the fishing industry has always and will always cause certain fisheries immense frustration.

Rail Transportation

The arrival of the railway was a tremendous advantage to Cornish fishermen. From 1859 the railways of Cornwall were connected to the national network of lines presenting a golden opportunity for the fisheries. Markets that were previously inaccessible opened up and new outlets became feasible. Fish could be packed at St Ives, Newlyn and Mousehole and kept fresh for markets in London and taken by train from Penzance. Stations at Truro, Par and

Liskeard served the fishing ports further up the line. Newlyn, Mousehole, Newquay and Padstow all had good natural harbours and piers which made offloading from the boats feasible and faster. The aim was to wash and pack the fish as soon as they were landed and get them to the fish train before it left Penzance. If they missed it, the fish would lose its shine and fail to be fresh enough to satisfy customers 'up country'.

Transporting fish by rail became a prosperous business enterprise with many companies competing throughout the region. It seemed as if prosperity would now come to the Cornish who made a living from the sea. The hand-to-mouth livelihood would be a thing of the past and the pilchard harvest no longer the most significant event of the year. Now fish could be transported all year round and seasonal fish transported with ease.

Dried, smoked and salted fish were also much-desired delicacies for those living in inland areas. Ling and cod were dried without too many complications, but rays and skates required careful treatment, as they were prone to releasing ammonia. Many were simply hung up outside the cottages in the streets and dried in the sun. Mackerel was often caught using hand-line methods, the simplicity of dropping a line underwater. The line would have ten to thirty hooks running down its length with lead weights at the end. Dropping a line off a fast-moving boat caught some fish, and sinking pots near to rocks caught crab and lobster. Pollack, bass and whiting were caught throughout the year and ling and cod during winter months.

Newquay's fishing fleet in 1904 at a time when rail links were essential for marketing catches further up country. The tramway is close to the mooring to speed up transportation procedures.

Hundreds of horse-drawn carts frequented the roads between fishing ports and rail links. Daily, throughout the year, these fish wagons were a vital connection between the fishermen and the railway. Ice from the Arctic was shipped in and stored in cellars and warehouses in the larger ports such as Newlyn. From the 1900s a way of freezing fresh water was mastered and ice was crushed and mixed with each packing case as a matter of course. Fish could then arrive at Billingsgate Market in peak condition.

However, not all fishing communities benefited from the rail links. Those that were isolated and less accessible, with poor roads preventing fast transportation, remained reliant on trade in the local area. Small fishing boats continued to work within remote coves and industrial fishing was centred in a few dominant ports.

Visiting drifters often made their way down from the North Sea. Fishermen from the north-east and even motor-powered trawlers from France began to invade the Cornishmen's fishing grounds. Groups of fishermen from other parts of the country competed for the same fish stocks. So it was necessary to invest in improved nets, faster trawlers and advanced equipment to outwit any rivals.

There will always be difficulties in the fishing industry. In an effort to conserve fish stocks there will, from time to time, be restrictions on catching certain species, such as cod or coley, and this can force fishermen to act against their better judgement. Sometimes the measures mean that banned fish inadvertently get brought to the surface with other mixed catches. The bottom-dwelling fish are often dead by the time they are brought up to the surface which means the dead, restricted fish then have to be thrown back into the water. The fishermen are left wondering about the wisdom of such practices when they see such unintended waste.

Shellfish

Fishing for crabs and lobsters has always been commonplace throughout Cornwall. Coves around the areas of Fowey, Mevagissey, Coverack, Cadgwith, Mullion, Prussia Cove, Penzance, St Just and Sennen all had crabbing luggers. Nowadays the pots that are used to capture crab, lobster and crayfish are mass-produced, made from steel, covered in plastics. In the past they were handmade using fine willow withies specially grown in marshes.

Over twenty crab or lobster pots were strung together, weighted by stones and dropped into the water. Bait such as mackerel or pilchards were used, attached to the mouth of the pots. It was obviously essential that a crew recorded the precise location of a fleet of pots so that it could be found

A collection of withy lobster pots on the quay at Porthleven in 1956. Now such objects are considered to be a quaint decoration, but before steel and plastic ones were introduced they served an entirely practical purpose.

again. Once the pots were positioned they could remain there for the season. They were visited twice a day so the crabs or lobsters could be collected and the pots re-baited.

Gathering cockles and mussels, or 'trigging', was also a way for local people to supplement their diets with shellfish from the shore. Limpets, cockles and mussels were traditionally eaten during Lent.

One form of fishing that today is carried out with traditional sailing fishing boats, is oyster fishing around the Fal estuary. Oyster dredging along a stretch of estuary known as the Carrick Roads near Falmouth has taken place for centuries and is the only oyster fishery in Europe to still use such traditional methods. Oysters are a luxury nowadays because of dwindling numbers due to over harvesting. However, the process of dredging along the sea bed, under sail or oars, has been consistent for hundreds of years and little has changed since the 1800s. Motorised dredgers are banned as they would seriously affect the stocks. There are strict conservation stipulations that determine the optimum size for retrieval. Although stocks can still be under-mined due to pollution and disease, using sail power and hand-pulled dredges the fishermen preserve the sensitive ecology of the area and also a dwindling fishing heritage.

In the seventeenth century there was a major oyster fishery at Saltash and they were often sold for export, many fishing boats making their way along the

*These cockle pickers were renowned for living in the caves at Downderrry,
south-east Cornwall, in 1906. The 'Downderry Cave Dwellers' were an
eccentric group of vagrants who survived from selling and consuming shellfish.*

estuary at high tide to transport their 'sea harvest' to the city of Plymouth.

The fifty years between the coming of the railway in 1859 and the end
of the nineteenth century witnessed the pinnacle of the Cornish fishing
trade. Higher prices could be achieved from hake, cod, mackerel and conger.
Since the 1900s the methods of catching fish have largely changed.
Traditional sailing luggers and labour-intensive rowing boats have been
superseded by motor-powered trawlers because sailing boats are no longer a
practical or economical method. Once drift boats started to be powered by

the internal combustion engine, it became possible to travel up to twenty miles away from port. The weather was less of a problem as the motor was not reliant on favourable wind conditions. As larger fishing grounds became more accessible, so shoals of fish were easier to come by and caught in greater numbers than by lugsail.

The handling of fish became more industrialised with packing and marketing of fresh fish involving more sophisticated road transportation facilities. The storing and freezing of stock meant that the curing of fish became less essential. As the industry has developed so have official guidelines. The fisheries will, it seems, always be subject to restrictions of one form or another and nowadays the economic viability of fishing continues to be in a precarious state. There continues to be controversy around different methods used and specific restrictions from government further compound a sense of complex contention within the industry.

No longer is it simply the ocean that the fishermen grapple with but also the political issues of our time. Yet it seems a life at sea has always been dogged by official strictures of one form or another. Since the seventeenth century there have been continuous tensions as tithes, taxes or strict fishing restrictions have been enforced. Each era has had its particular issues of contention as the fisherman has needed to heed official stipulations.

Newlyn

Newlyn has always been a fishing village first and foremost and it was to become the main port in the South West. Newlyn's deep-sea fisherman's main objective has always been to return safely to the harbour with a full catch for the auctioneers. His family and friends would be constantly mindful of him being away at sea, watching the horizon periodically, anxious for a vessel's safe return. The higgledy-piggledy cottages and walkways are still to this day home to a community accustomed to hardship and tragedy at sea. Many fishermen over the years have drowned and their boats lost. This has not been due to ignorance necessarily, but more to daring and courage, having to take a risk to bring a full net home.

In more recent history, Newlyn caused a national stir following a radical reform in the Housing Act of 1936, which deemed many fishermen's cottages 'unfit for human habitation'. Compulsory Purchase Orders stated intent to demolish whole streets around the harbour, so the national newspapers took up the alarmed residents' plight. The debate between those officials with aspirations for progress and those who wanted to preserve their homes were voiced. Health inspectors were brought in to scrutinise the

Two typical street scenes in Newlyn circa 1903. The need for restoration and repair of the buildings is indicative of the lack of care from landlords rather than the tenant fishermen. It was streets such as these that were considered to be unfit for human habitation.

lives and practices of fishermen's families, and their way of life was often considered to be unhygienic.

Row upon row of tiny cottages housed the fishing communities. Stone-built dwellings of all shapes and sizes crammed together, many sharing yards, baking facilities and water pumps. Some homes had a Cornish range or open fire, others benefited from piped water, but all took advantage of any available space, and any sort of garden area was a luxury. These tiny homes were crowded to full capacity. Once they would have reeked with the stench of fish and the silver scales would glisten like glitter on the floorboards. These were homes whose whole focus was the sea. The lamps would burn fish oil as the nets were drying in the covered yard outside.

Many generations lived next to each other. The streets would have been a jumble of drying washing and children playing. Keeping homes clean in such conditions would have been a persistent struggle. There was little privacy, yet such closeness meant nobody's needs went unseen. It may have been squalid in some places, and often far from ideal, but nobody went hungry for long, there was little crime and everybody bore life's hardships together. There may have been differences in living standards throughout the village, from those affluent skippers and boat owners to the poorest workers with large families to provide for, but they were all united in their service to the one great master of them all, the sea.

Often homes were almost entirely given over to processing fish in some way or other, or used as a space to store nets and crates. Yet despite the ever-present smell of fish, these homes could arguably be said to have been healthier than those of the inner cities. Admittedly there was poverty and depravation, and tenants mostly inhabited the properties that the council recommended for demolition. They were deemed to be beyond repair and as there was no notion of preserving the past or conserving historical charm, the authorities were intent on wide-scale demolition.

Whether there was justification to consider these dwellings as sub-standard and irredeemable against strict hygiene criteria is debatable. It seems likely that with considered strategies it would have been possible to preserve these streets. Maybe if sanitation had been introduced then effective improvements could have been made. Certainly areas that avoided being cleared stand as desirable homes today. These areas were originally marked by inspectors for tearing down.

Despite the valiant protest from the crew of the vessel *Rosebud*, who sailed to Parliament, the demolition of many homes took place between 1937 and 1940. Areas in places such as Bowjey Hill, Fradgan Place and St Peter's Place were destroyed. Those who were made homeless were relocated to the Gwavas, a new council-housing complex higher up on the hill close to the countryside surrounding Paul. Admittedly there was more space; each home had a garden and running water. However, the community that existed before was dispersed and extended families separated when they were allocated new homes next to strangers. Despite the upheaval there were those who were grateful to move out of the sometimes damp and dismal dwellings close to the harbour, while others grieved the loss of their previous homes.

The *Rosebud* voyage certainly slowed the whole housing reform process down. The widespread demolitions originally intended were not carried out in full, and it was the south part of Newlyn that was most affected. Partly also due to the start of the war, the slum clearances were postponed and in peacetime were never reintroduced. The 1930s' vision for a grand concrete scheme never materialised and although some houses were lost for good, other supposed 'slums' have been sensitively restored and survive today.

Newlyn's slipway between the Old Quay and South Pier as it was in 1947. Above the areas of Fore Street, Newlyn Town, North Corner and Street-an-Nowan were no longer under threat from 'slum' clearance. These buildings stand today thanks to the Rosebud *and a decision to cease demolition during the war.*

It could well be that, because of the *Rosebud's* intervention, the neighbouring, picturesque village of Mousehole has remained fully intact. Any visionary mass clearances that were hinted at were likely reconsidered in the light of the public outcry following the *Rosebud's* protest.

Many aspects of a fisherman's life remain unchanged yet others are unrecognisable when compared to the past. Newlyn's streets still smell of fish and the seagulls are ever-present pests to those who work on the trawlers. To some, the place has a rough reputation; hardened individuals need to face the cruelty of the sea's forces daily. Fishermen whose hands are made red raw from being in and out of freezing salt water and the faces of young men aged prematurely by the salt spray and sun display their catches in the early morning auctions each day. This place has a timeless charm, a workaday authenticity that is resilient despite those aspects of Cornish fishing that have gone.

Newlyn today is the predominant fishing port of Cornwall. The difficulties faced are connected to the stringent fishing quotas being enforced by

*Newlyn's fish market in 1931 had a distinct sense of the past, yet early
morning auctions, in many ways not too dissimilar to this,
are carried out in Newlyn today.*

European Union regulators. This kind of preventative measure is reminiscent
of times past when Parliament intervened in the 1800s between the seine and
drift fisheries, causing tension and conflict. However, now there is a very
real threat as the situation presents a possibility of utter financial ruin for the
remaining crews of smaller boats. The Common Fisheries Policy on strict
catch quotas means that fishermen are unable to land their catches and worse
still, have to throw back already dead fish, such as cod, because they die in
the nets before they are brought to the surface. In the past inshore trawler-
men could swap between several types of fishing depending on the season.
Now fishermen are tied into a certain type of fishing and restrained by
regulations aimed at conserving dwindling stocks.

Despite the fact that a fisherman's life was always, and will always be
a hard fight against both the elements and the regulatory bodies, there is
nevertheless a stubborn and stoical determination to carry on. There is a
remnant of the fishing industry that persists and the current generation continues to strive to survive and even thrive, still devoted to the fishing tradition.

CHAPTER 5

THE NEWLYN SCHOOL

It was in Newlyn that Stanhope Forbes, the Victorian realist painter, decided to settle. The workaday village with its remarkable sweeping bay that looks out to St Michael's Mount and the Lizard Point in the distance has a different mood with each change of wind condition and turning of the tide. The ocean is never the same, the colours of the sea and sky always altering with the shifting sunlight. The dazzling blue of a summer's day with the twinkle of sunshine glinting off each ripple of the water contrasts with the bleak grey of a winter storm, the skyline obliterated by the murky sea mist. It was nature in all its diversity that inspired Forbes, but it was also the characters within a scene that captivated his fascination too.

Nowadays Forbes's work could be dismissed by some as being overly quaint with little aesthetic appeal to the modern art connoisseur. Forbes doesn't present the brutality of life at sea or grapple with the pain that accompanied the livelihoods in some of his pastoral scenes. He was eager to represent the scenic. His work is enchanting and endearing, presenting a view of Cornish life that is predominantly pleasant. Whether somebody favours his style or not, there can be little argument that he convincingly conveys something of Cornwall's past. Aspects of Cornish culture, now lost, have been indelibly documented, and he offers us informative insights into the late 1800s and early 1900s.

Since Forbes's day other art movements have arrested the critics' and collectors' consideration and new visions have become dominant. Now Forbes's paintings are reproduced on birthday cards, boxes of fudge for tourists, and are representative of a bygone era in art history. It could be argued that his was 'a time when artists knew how to draw'. There was nothing of the impressionist or abstract in his work but rather the painstaking application of realist principles. His was a style rooted in the recreation of what was present before him in nature. Yet his work and that of his Newlyn associates needs to be recognised as the radical pioneering pieces they were.

Stanhope Forbes at his easel, painting Off to the Fishing Grounds, *circa 1886.*

Their fresh approach was considered by many critics of their day as being progressive and even revolutionary.

Forbes's first visit to Cornwall was early in 1884 when he left London intending to spend several months painting in Penwith around the Land's End peninsula. However, it only took only a day's visit to Newlyn, as he wrote to his mother, before he determined to settle in the village. He described his first thoughts on reaching Newlyn on that day in a local publication called *The Cornish Magazine*. This article entitled 'Newlyn Retrospect' was written fifteen years after the event, in 1899, and reveals much of Forbes's thinking and motivation concerning his work and his reasoning behind settling in the village. Extracts of this precious article, edited by A. T. Quiller-Couch have been included throughout this chapter as they are too insightful to leave unshared.

Forbes begins the article by writing:

I had come from France where I had been studying, and, wandering down into Cornwall, came one spring morning along the dusty road by which Newlyn is approached from Penzance. Little did I think that the cluster of grey-roofed houses, which I saw against the hill, would be my home for so many years.

Yet contemporary opinion did not necessarily share the favourable view that Forbes fostered for Newlyn. H. Besley's *Handbook of Western Cornwall* was written in 1852, a couple of decades before Forbes and his associates had begun to settle in what became known as the Newlyn Colony. It wasn't until their work was exhibited and gained national significance that the village was considered to be worthy of note. Besley writes: 'There is nothing worthy of particular attention in the town of Newlyn excepting those objects of interest which are necessarily connected with its fishing operations.'

It is interesting that Forbes considered there to be a lifetime's work of interest in the village and, indeed, there proved to be enough to attract his attention and absorb him and hundreds of painters since. It was perhaps the beauty of the coast and Forbes's love of outdoor painting that strongly influenced his decision to work in such a geographically remote place. He was part of a group of artists, many of whom had spent time in France and revered working out of doors 'en plein air' rather than creating tableaus within a studio space. Even Constable, so great a landscape painter, made sketches out of doors but worked on the canvas indoors. Forbes was motivated to study humanity against the backdrop of natural surroundings and his paintings are sympathetic to those who worked out in the elements.

These students from Paris and Antwerp started to meet after they returned to England and began to live and work closely together forming artists' colonies. They were admiring of the work of Jules Bastien-Lepage who exhibited *Les Foins* in 1878 and *Joan of Arc* a year later. These works are considered to be the foundation of the plein-air movement.

Several of these colonies sprang up all over Britain during the 1880s; they were supportive communities of known and lesser-known artists. Just a few miles away in St Ives another group of artists were living alongside each other and this included such names as Anders Zorn who also gained international significance. The Newlyn Art Colony was part of an international movement that was partly rebelling against the strictures and traditions of art academia. They broke with convention by painting and living in rural areas taking working subjects as their main inspiration.

Generally in the 1870s and 1880s French Arts became more influential and as a consequence the New English Art Club (NEAC) was founded. Forbes became strongly affiliated with the NEAC, as his approach was more akin to their philosophies and methods. This was to be more of a movement that artists could affiliate to, rather than a coherent institution. Individual artists who were inspired by French ideas could associate with the club, while drawing on a wider range of influences in their work. Many English artists were traditional in their approach to landscape or figure painting and favoured the plein-air style while others in the NEAC were propagating impressionist ideals. It was the French influence that made its way down to Newlyn in various guises. Despite Forbes distancing himself from the Royal Academy of Arts it didn't preclude him from being honoured as a Royal Academician in 1910.

It was within colonies in France that younger artists painted together during the summer months under the guidance of an established proficient. It was therefore unsurprising that similar colonies started to form once the students returned to English shores. Walter Langley and Edwin Harris were the first to pioneer such a colony at Newlyn and it was with these first settlers that Forbes was to align himself and in many ways come to lead. Other Newlyn artists who preferred to brace the Cornish air were Percy Craft, Norman Garstin, Thomas Cooper Gotch, Ralph Todd, Harold Harvey, Samuel John, Lamorna Birch, Harold Knight, Dame Laura Knight, Dod Procter, Ernest Procter, Henry Meynell Rheam, and Charles W. Simpson. Forbes was to meet his wife Elizabeth (née Armstrong) in the village.

When the artists first arrived in Newlyn they headed for the more prosperous areas of the village up on the hillside, away from the intense fishy smell of the quay and fish market. Many seemed to have initially lodged with Mrs Maddern, who offered lodgings in Belle Vue. She had a very strong opinion concerning painting on the sabbath and would not allow any of her paying guests to touch a brush on a Sunday.

It wasn't just painting that drew the Newlyn artists together but a sense of community and belonging. Music and acting were very much part of their everyday lives together, as were informal gatherings in each other's homes and studios. There seems to have been a strong sense of companionship as they congregated to share ideas and resources.

Forbes remembers the early days of the Newlyn Colony with fondness:

I like to recall those early days in the history of the colony, when, starting our careers full of enthusiasm and hope, so many of us came together and formed fast friendships, when the comradeship which still exists was solidly founded.

There were many non-conformist Christian villagers who were shocked by the artists' bohemian lifestyle and, although tolerated, there was nevertheless strong disapproval from many and some took great exception to their setting up huge canvases, attracting crowds of curious onlookers, when they could have been in chapel. Yet they accepted each other's differences and the artists' colony became an integral part of the village.

Once they became known, Newlyn was presented rather differently in the guidebooks of the day as this extract from *The Netherton and Worth Tourists' Guide To Cornwall* in 1900 illustrates:

Newlyn, with its quaint streets, picturesque fisher-folk and beautiful situation, is the home of a school of artists well known to the general public. The Passmore Edwards Art gallery, the gift of the generous Cornishman whose name it bears, is a fine building of stone and granite. Exhibitions of pictures by the Newlyn and St Ives artists are frequently held there.

The Newlyn artists strove to portray the rigours, hardships and pleasures of living in a Cornish fishing village and in the surrounding countryside. The most renowned work was produced during the 1880s and 1890s when many of the paintings were successfully received into public exhibitions and prized by private collectors.

Artists on the cliff, Newlyn. Left to right: unknown, Walter Langley, Percy Craft, Frank Bodily (seated).

There was a prevailing nostalgic ideology that rural life was to be regarded as admirable and even preferable to city life. It was considered that traditional country ways were able to provide answers to the ills of urban industrialisation and needed to be preserved and honoured through art. Many artists deemed it imperative to live alongside their subjects, gaining inspiration from everyday work activities and representing the immediacy of observation through their painting. It was only by living among the occupants of Newlyn that the artists could faithfully document their lives. Despite the cultural differences the villagers respected the accuracy and painstaking recording in oil paint. It was due to these paintings that this little village gained a measure of fame well beyond the Tamar.

Authenticity to a point was depicted, although often the more offensive, harsh and unsightly realities were deliberately omitted depending on whether the artist wished to represent political and social overtones or not. There tended to be a romantic interpretation of the efforts of manual labour, and daily life for the poor and struggling. Even the tragic, when viewed from today's perspective, was depicted in a melodramatic and stylised form, tending towards the picturesque rather than the gruelling.

Newlyn in the late 1800s offered the gutsy life of the fishing community.

Forbes derived his inspiration from the ordinary folk of the village. He was motivated by their practical tasks, the rustic elements of their livelihood, and yet he had the ability to identify and recreate the scenic in what he saw. He was able to discern how light played on the mundane in life and how it had the capacity to bring vitality and vivacity to a scene. Although Forbes was working among those who were hardened to poverty, and who faced grave adversity from the stormy waters, this harshness was presented in a pleasing way as if he saw the world as entirely charming and delightful.

There is no denying that his work evokes a sense of nostalgia. He depicts a time that has passed and in many ways it would be easy to become over sentimental about certain aspects. Although he had a startling skill shown in the clarity and precision of his figures – demonstration of an almost photographic ability – he nevertheless embellished all he painted with enchantment and a childlike delight.

Forbes had a keen desire to study humanity within out-of-doors surroundings. In particular, he considered it to be of the utmost importance to experience all aspects of nature, to familiarise himself with the landscape and people in it. He was of the opinion that it was essential to exist within the scene he painted and to study every part of it closely. To this end he would set up his easel under the open sky and brave the weather to capture the everyday experiences around him. His main concerns were with the affairs of Newlyn's villagers and simple happenings in their lives. His work conveys a sincere respect for those he chose to paint and he demonstrated an admiration for them not only visually but socially too. His sea was not that of the traditional landscape painter but he saw it through the eyes of the seamen. He was renowned for painting honestly, meticulous in his desire to capture the subtleties of atmosphere.

Forbes put down his remembrances of his early ideals:

Yes those were the days of unflinching realism, of the cult of Bastien-Lepage. It was part of our artistic creed to paint our pictures directly from nature, and not merely to rely upon sketches and studies which we could afterwards amplify in the comfort of a studio.

He attempted to record what he saw rather than rely on memory or composing from sittings in a studio. He afforded the humble worker with the same level of respect that he had previously bestowed on the wealthy, distinguished or socially esteemed. By focusing on the ordinary in humanity a statement of worth was clearly being made: he was bestowing honour on to common mankind. Recognition of value was being placed on those who were generally considered to be of a lower social order. As he explains:

> The people intelligently grasped the idea that there was nothing derogatory to their dignity in being painted – indeed, saw and felt the implied compliment.
>
> And what better material could artists have wished for? A fine-knit race of men and women, engaged in a healthy and picturesque occupation, and one which by its nature gives the painter his opportunity, when storms and tempests arise, to secure the necessary sittings, swarms of children, many of them charmingly pretty; no wonder that enough material has been found to keep us engaged these many years.

There were many changes taking place in the art scene when Forbes began to paint in Newlyn. A range of ideas affected the artists from the late 1860s up to the 1880s. There were still those who held on to Classicism and Pre-Raphaelite principles, or who were part of the Aesthetic movement, but there were also those who were emerging from this era, experimenting with the Realist approach. There was a strong pioneering element driven to paint straightforward landscape scenes and also those who were inspired to capture the human subject within an environmental context. Many of these works either told a story or portrayed a social message.

There was no adamant revolutionary talk voiced by Forbes against the established conventions in the academic institutions and tastes of the time; it was more of an instinctive reaction. Above all, he aimed, and enthused so that other artists followed, to paint each work from the beginning to the end out of doors.

He had a need to work directly from nature and there were other English painters who were inclined to do likewise.

It was Forbes's painting entitled *The Fish Sale on a Cornish Beach* that gained him and his Cornish work recognition and high praise, particularly from critics in the Royal Academy in 1885. The painting is now representative of an entire era in Cornish history and is upheld as being entirely evocative of a life in the fisheries. The painting depicts a couple of Newlyn women in the foreground, with a catch of fish laid out on the wet sand. They are talking to a mackerel fisherman and in the distance, close to the seashore we see a group of villagers crowding around a mule and cart and more fish laid out for sale. Old fishing luggers are sailing out in the bay, their tawny brown sails on

Stanhope Forbes painting in Boase Street, Newlyn, in the 1880s.

the horizon. The silver, grey light in the painting has a profoundly brilliant quality, despite the muted tones of colour. The expressive faces of the figures and the poignancy of movement tells a dramatic tale of life in a fishing village.

Forbes recalls that first moment of awe as he viewed the light reflecting of the wet sand near Werrytown:

> From the first I was fascinated by those wet sands, with their groups of figures reflected on the shiny surface, which the auctioneer's bell would gather around him for the barter of his wares. If you look back now to Penzance you will see, stretching out far into the bay, the sands at low tide. It was there that I elected to paint my first Newlyn picture, and out on that exposed beach, for many a month, struggled over a large canvas. I blush to recall what my models must have suffered posing for these early works of mine, and am only consoled by so often meeting healthy strapping lasses, or bronzed-faced young fishermen, whom I can remember as children shivering on the beach or roasting in the August sun whilst a young and over-zealous painter, forgetting all but his work, wrestled with the difficulties of light and shade.

The Fish Sale on a Cornish Beach was to lead the way for others and it was perhaps this alone that established Forbes as the 'Father' of the Newlyn artists. He led by his commitment to his art; his diligent, relentless output. He had studiously attended all the best schools of the time and had applied himself to painting a series of portraits, six of which were exhibited at the Royal Academy. In many ways he had a disciplined and systematic approach to his work and the other, less successful artists followed his example. However, he was also relishing the release of painting outside; for him this was a kind of revelry.

It was the character of a subject that he sought, fisherfolk whose faces and hands had been marred by hard work and sea air. His pursuit was to recreate the truth from the features before him, indifferent at times to their unsightliness, making them offer vitality with the play of light. Despite sometimes being uncouth these characters were dominant in all Forbes's paintings and he specialised in crafting realistic hands and faces.

Forbes considered it imperative to seek out every changing mood of the day, the shadows and sunlight, and to capture each movement in exacting detail, to study the way light behaved on land and sea. He was interested in how any interior lamplight was affected by daylight coming in through windows. He had an obsession with light. He was to become a master of painting light rather than colour with pale sunshine and shades of grey portrayed in his early Newlyn work. However, as paints started to be sold ready mixed in tubes, it became no longer necessary to mix them from pigments on a palette out of doors, so the practicalities of using a range of colours was easier. Forbes's *Haycart* of 1903 and his *February Sunshine* testify to him being an effectual colourist also.

Painting out of doors in this way was a painstaking and complex procedure requiring days and weeks of patience. Not only would the awkward-shaped and weighty easel and stool have to be carried to a location but the paints needed to be mixed on the palette out of doors too. This had to happen in wind and threatening drizzle, with an ever-changing light causing extra pressure on the artist's time. It was about this time that inventive local builders came up with the idea of making glass studios for the artists. Several were built rather like conservatories, sometimes mobile and portable, so that the painters could appreciate the Newlyn light without being hindered by the sea mist and drizzle. Forbes had one for his use. He sounds mildly amused as he reflects on his profession:

> It is a debatable practice, and this is no place to argue such technicalities, but I mention it because, being strongly held by many of us, it imparted a noticeable feature to the village. Artists are common enough objects by the seaside; but it was scarcely so usual to see the painter not merely engaged upon a small sketch or panel, but with a large canvas securely fastened to some convenient boulder, absorbed in the very work with which he hoped to win fame in the ensuing spring; perhaps even a model posing in full view of the entire populace, the portrait being executed with a publicity calculated to unnerve even our practiced brother artist of the pavement.

Forbes had a frank and forthright style and a confidence in what he wanted to achieve. Because he always painted 'on the spot', believing this was the essential element in capturing atmosphere, conditions were sometimes prohibitive and must have led to much discomfort. One such occasion was when he painted his famous oil on canvas *Forging The Anchor* in 1892. He spent the entire time coping with heat from the furnace, noise, dust and smoke that all seemed to conspire against him.

However, it was his painting of *The Smithy* that gained him a Gold Medal in Munich and another at the Paris International Exhibition in 1899.

He recalled a particular moment during its execution as if walking around the top of Paul Hill in his head:

> Passing through this little hamlet I can point out a smithy, in the smoke and grime of which, working for months, I managed to carry to completion a large picture; and further on by the roadside a spot where one day I was forced to snatch up a seven-foot canvas, and, leaping a hedge, fly before a herd of advancing cattle.

The residents of Newlyn evidently came to accept these clusters of bohemians in their midst over time. By all accounts these artistic settlers received a kindly reception by the majority as they carried out their creative occupations openly in full view of all passers-by. The artists coexisted peaceably in the streets on the quayside, spreading out easel and painting utensils, fully focused on their observation of those inhabitants working nearby, as Forbes testifies:

> When one considers the interest aroused by our proceedings, it speaks well for the good nature of the village folk that I can scarcely ever remember asking permission to set up my easel without it being freely accorded.

The fishermen were the main focus of attention and there was no ill feeling as the artists were afforded a measure of respect for their ability to recreate what they saw. For it was the weather-beaten and fish-stained unpretentious individuals that the artists longed to capture on canvas and who they evidently found co-operative as Forbes writes:

> Indeed, it is fortunate for us that the relations of the artist to the villagers have always been so cordial and satisfactory. A well-known portrait painter is said to have observed that he counted as many enemies as he had painted portraits. Luckily this feeling does not exist here, else were the lot of some of us an unenviable one. Scores of the village folk, young and old, women and children, have sat to us and bear no malice – indeed.

Student Days
Born in 1857 in Dublin, Stanhope Alexander Forbes was brought up by his father, manager of the Irish railway, and his French mother. His father,

William, had cultivated high-brow literary tastes and therefore encouraged his son from an early age and throughout his student life to read works by great writers such as Dickens, Hardy, Carlyle and Thackery. But it was his mother, Juliette de Guise, to whom he was especially close. He wrote to her frequently after he left home to discuss many of his plans and successes, describing his life in great detail. She was a devoted friend to her son and a great influence, encouraging him throughout his adult life and visiting him and his wife, Elizabeth, at Newlyn. Countless locals in Newlyn village remembered the senior Mr Forbes, in particular. He had a reputation of being popular with the children and was known to be fond of every kind of animal.

Maybe it was his careful parenting that instilled such a sensitive and sympathetic nature within Stanhope, although some have hinted that it was another incident in childhood that would make for a tender persona. At the age of 5 or 6 he was taken aboard HMS *Resistance* with his parents while it was docked in Dublin Bay. Unfortunately as a sailor was carrying him he slipped and Stanhope was lost overboard in the sea. A dramatic rescue ensued and he was returned to his distraught parents on the shore, unconscious but alive. Throughout his life he was troubled by ailments that his family considered to be linked to this experience. Despite his so-called delicate health and sensitive nature he went on to live an active and fruitful life until he died at the age of 89.

Both parents were proud of their son's artistic success; they had invested much in his education, particularly encouraging him to pursue his love of drawing and painting. Forbes was fortunate to have the continued support of his parents and their substantial wealth behind him throughout his novice years. Initially a governess taught him and his elder brother William at home in Ireland. But then the family all moved to London and the boys went to Dulwich College to be educated. It was here that Stanhope came under the instruction of the art master, John Sparkes, who employed enlightened methods of teaching drawing. Instead of the painstaking and 'mindless' copying of other artists' works, he roused in his pupils an interest to draw from cast models. Stanhope found this activity particularly absorbing and was said to have missed many playtimes, preferring to sketch instead. It was this chosen activity that was to make his time at school so gratifying.

Most significant to his creative development was a family holiday in the Ardennes where the young Forbes was to make the acquaintance of the three Misses Harrison. The sisters were on a sketching tour and took a genuine interest in the 11-year-old Stanhope. They encouraged his aptitude by allowing him to accompany them on drawing excursions and no doubt offered him some useful advice. Miss Maria, in particular, was a member of the Old Water Colour Society and took much notice of the young boy. His first drawing was of *The Old Chateau and Village of Rochefort*. This little ensemble of artists were to become lasting friends and met up on later similar trips, a notable one being in Scotland.

Stanhope's father was aware of his son's desire to draw and it was perhaps due to his careful oversight that he realised his ambition to become a professional artist. William Forbes approached Stanhope's former art master, Sparkes, who became headmaster of South Kensington School of Art, for some scholarly advice. Together they looked at Stanhope's sketchbook and it was decided that the young man should be allowed to follow his vocation. From then on he studied at Lambeth School compiling a portfolio of work of a sufficient standard to compete and be accepted at the Royal Academy Schools.

The Royal Academy, founded in the eighteenth century, was the most prestigious institution in Victorian art culture. Its summer exhibition was the start of the season in London and was considered to have been a highly desirable and fashionable event to attend.

At the Academy Schools Stanhope was influenced and instructed by some of the most influential painters of his time. He was to study alongside Solomon J. Solomon, Arthur Hacker and La Thangue. It is worth considering that the nineteenth century saw some of England's most distinguished painters accomplish genius works. It was the 'golden' century that saw the likes of Turner, Millais, Rossetti, Holman and Albert Joseph Moore gain ascendancy and recognition.

Forbes and a fellow student, Hacker, from the Academy Schools went on to study in France together. The celebrated portrait painter, Léon Bonnat, mentored them. At Clichy he found himself among a range of nationalities where he was exposed to various techniques and influences. The days in Bonnat's studio were full working days and tens of students worked alongside each other creating a great hubbub. However, this only served to instill in him an individual instinct, which he diligently pursued. He went on to hire his own studio space and began to adopt a plein-air method, looking to others besides Bonnat for guidance and approval. It was at this time that he moved away from the safety of portrait painting and experimented painting his first pieces partly out of doors. He was anxious that both his mother and the British public would appreciate what he produced, and they did. *A Street In Brittany* was bought by Liverpool Gallery in 1882 and it was this positive response in particular that encouraged him to branch out and take the step of becoming an outdoor painter.

He kept determinedly to his own chosen path and demonstrated much conviction in identifying and developing his own talent. He was never satisfied until he captured exactly what he was observing. It was not enough to portray a general likeness; he upheld the principle of exactness and shunned any concept of falsification. Determined to get to the heart of things he would study every line and tone intently to ensure that he gained a realistic rendering. Forbes's robust academic training had instilled the best Victorian traditions and methods in his work. Yet despite the conventional compositions, he had been strongly influenced by the softer, almost impressionist style of painting from his trips in France.

It was his deep love for his adopted home of Newlyn that was to prove the most influential aspect of his work. He rarely left throughout his working life, such was his affection for the way of life, the community of artists and his respect for the Newlyners. He saw something in their ability to cope with the joys, sorrows and hardships, as well as their determination to overcome, as something of lasting value and it was this he endeavoured to record for posterity.

The School

Cornish journalist and owner of several newspapers, John Passmore Edwards, commissioned a number of public buildings throughout the Duchy. Such was his conviction that education and gaining knowledge were of immense value to society that he funded schools and libraries for common use. One such project was the founding of a 'Newlyn School' and the artists welcomed his proposal, even if a few of the locals did not take to the idea. The first exhibition was in October 1895 and it was at this stage that Forbes became the acknowledged leader of the other members. His gratitude to Passmore Edwards is evident in this extract:

> But when fate in the person of Mr. Passmore Edwards decreed that we should possess an art gallery, it became inevitable that the pictures could no longer be exhibited in this novel manner, and seeing the many advantages which the possession of a properly constructed exhibition room has conferred upon us, it were ungenerous to cavil at so small a matter.
>
> It was a kind and generous thought of the giver to bestow this admirable little gallery upon us, and not the less gratifying for being so entirely spontaneous and unsought for. The success it has met with so far, not only from the support which the public of West

Cornwall has given it, but those panels of beaten copper on the façade are worth noticing. They are a product of the place, one of the latest developments of Newlyn art.

Forbes had always set up private lessons where he lectured and gave criticism to his pupils' work. He particularly enjoyed the stimulation of being with younger artists and they benefited from his encouragement and sympathetic guidance. So it was merely a gradual progression to take on a prominent role at the new school. Forbes was to be the driving force behind the school in its early history and he was optimistic about its future. He saw it entirely as a public institution and shied away from any notion that it was an exclusive artists' club. Anybody could become a member for a fee and the artists held classes. Forbes held sessions on drawing and painting from life and landscape painting. Harold Harvey and Ernest Procter covered still life and decoration, whilst Charles W. Simpson and his wife instructed students on figure, marine and animal painting.

Classes were intended for those who had a serious interest in painting or who considered it to be their life's vocation. The instructors were determined not to have their students slavishly follow their example, rather, the intention was to prevent their students experiencing the same pitfalls as them. They shared method but encouraged independence of thought as well as experimentation, imparting to the next generation of artists a firm artistic base from which to explore.

The school building, now called The Newlyn Art Gallery, has an extraordinary history in that it has gained such pre-eminence for such an isolated and small locality. Art that previously would have only made it to the larger national galleries was exhibited there for the first time. It is unlikely that all the residents were aware of the significance of some of these pieces or indeed of the importance of some of the names in their midst. Visitors from all over the globe travelled down for a rare glimpse, or to purchase some of most influential contributions to the history of art.

Both Stanhope Forbes and his wife Elizabeth exhibited in Newlyn School's first exhibition among other artists, and twenty-three pictures were sold on that occasion. The couple continued to exhibit at Newlyn, the Royal Academy and in other galleries. Elizabeth's paintings and sketches were always popular and sold well wherever she exhibited.

Forbes was considered to be the 'artist par excellence' among his contemporaries in Newlyn, and although others produced outstanding work, his was the standard to which theirs was compared. Despite his teaching commitments, he continued to produce a prolific output of paintings as well, including numerous portraits.

Newlyn continued to be an important artistic centre well into the twentieth century, even though some of the original artist settlers returned to London or France. A particularly successful year for the Newlyn School was 1911 when the work of the Cornish School was esteemed by the Tate Gallery. This included the work of Stanhope Forbes, Frank Bramley and Thomas Cooper Gotch.

Elizabeth Forbes

In many ways Elizabeth Forbes suffered from the social status of women of her era; she lived in the shadow of her husband. This was exacerbated by his being so famous and successful. Before her marriage she contributed to sixty-three major London exhibitions, but only eight afterwards. It was unfortunate that she lived at a time when it was widely considered unseemly for a married woman to be a professional artist. It is interesting to note that it was not until 1882 that a second Married Women's Property Act was recognised, which for the first time legislated that women should have the same rights over their property as their husbands and could carry on trades and businesses using their separate interest in the property. It was not until 1919 that the Sex Disqualification Removal Act made it unlawful to bar women from public office. This was the climate in which Elizabeth was working. It would not be until some time after both their deaths that the Equal Pay Act was established in 1970. When reflecting on these facts alone it is evident that Elizabeth was not treated with the same esteem and credibility as her husband and other male artists in the colony once she married. The author would dare to suggest that it had nothing to do with the quality of her work; far from it.

By comparison Stanhope, over a nineteen-year period, participated in forty-two principal London shows, a significant difference between both their achievements, yet it was Stanhope that gained most acclaim. Despite Stanhope's advantage in Victorian society, Elizabeth nevertheless produced more work than him, something that is rarely recognised.

In general the plight of all Victorian women artists was to be subjected to a relative lack of recognition by male critics compared to their male contemporaries. Determined in her vocation, supported by her tutors and her mother especially, as a single woman Elizabeth struggled despite all to become an esteemed artist in her own right. She had already produced, what are still considered to be masterpieces, by the time she met her husband: *The Zandvoort Fisher Girl* was painted the year before she first met Stanhope in 1885.

Elizabeth Forbes in her studio in the 1880s.

By the time the young couple met, Stanhope was twenty-eight years old and this was to be his first serious relationship with a woman. There was some opposition from his mother, but she had a three-year-long engagement to get used to the idea. It may have been Elizabeth's lack of moneyed background, or even the fact that being an artist was considered to be an unsuitable occupation for a woman. Whatever her reason, her son's enthusiasm and devotion to his fiancée won his mother round. He was full of praise for Elizabeth's industrious nature and achievements in the art world.

Born in Canada in 1859, Elizabeth Adela Armstrong was her parents' youngest child and spent many childhood hours reading and retreating from the activities of her older siblings. It was perhaps these years that gave her an appreciation of a child's imagination for she was to become enraptured by the theme of childhood in her later work.

In her teens she left with her mother to be schooled in London and attended Kensington Art School. She returned briefly to Canada after her father's death, then went on to New York where she was part of the Students' League of New York. In 1881 the Royal Institute of Painters acknowledged three of her watercolours and she was accepted into membership two years later. She lived in London with her uncle and was accompanied everywhere by her mother. Together they travelled to Munich, Brittany and Holland, where Elizabeth was exposed to a range of artistic influences.

Elizabeth had regular exhibitions at the Royal Institute and sold pictures at the British Artists' galleries and some of her etchings at the Royal Academy. Stanhope did not particularly encourage or approve of her etching and it is possible this had something to do with her connection with one of her tutors, Walter Sickert. In spite of him being a celebrated artist, he was also notorious for frequenting brothels and used scenes from bars with spurious reputations as his subject matter. Even though this lifestyle was typical of many artists, Stanhope was a deeply conventional man with Victorian reserves. He had a strong aversion to Sickert's work and lifestyle, and made his disapproval of him and his associates, including Whistler, known to his future bride. Yet despite Stanhope's lack of support, Elizabeth continued to work on her etchings until she was married, at which time her work in that media ceased. One cannot help but read into the situation that she bent to his will and influence as a dutiful wife.

Her particular genre was to capture the domestic activities and lives of women and, especially, children. It was during her stay in Brittany in the early 1800s that she first discovered a love and remarkable aptitude for painting childhood pastimes.

The Apple Pickers is one of Elizabeth's oils on canvas, painted in 1883. Three children, dressed in delightful Victorian costume, are amiably picking apples together. Of particular note is the strong red she has introduced by including geraniums, which tie into the exact shade of the bright red sash of one of the girls. It is a delightful scene of idyllic playtime pursuits in a rural setting, evocative of a romantised Victorian simplicity.

One of her most notable pieces is School is Out, a scene of Paul village school in 1888 when she was still single. This charming piece captures the woman's world. Teaching children of primary age was predominantly a woman's role in the Victorian era, and the scene of the classroom is full of female concerns. There is one teacher still seated at her desk and another guiding the children out through the open door. A group of children are gathered together in a friendly huddle while a boy, evidently upset, remains sitting on the bench, perhaps having been reprimanded for some misdemeanour. The detail is extraordinary, from the expressions on the children's faces to the colours and textures of their clothes. She uses the light from two sources, the window and the open door, to suggest a sunny day outside. There is a softness to her work contrasting with the harsher naturalism and more lucid lines of her husband's painting. But like him she had a genuine sympathy for her subjects as she painted children taking part in a range of everyday activities.

Much later she also illustrated and wrote the words for a stunning book, King Arthur's Wood, published in 1904. Produced in a Pre-Raphaelite style she dedicated it to the couple's son, Alec. She excelled in her ability to visually capture light and movement.

Initially Elizabeth preferred St Ives to Newlyn and she chose to spend considerable time during her engagement away from Stanhope in a rented studio in the other fishing village. This caused some contention as Stanhope refused to mingle with the cosmopolitan crowd in her set and was determined to stay put. Evidently he won her around in the end, but not before she had spent several independent months near Carbis Bay.

However, in the book written in 1906 by her friend, Mrs Lionel Birch, there is a descriptive piece by Elizabeth that is full of admiring adjectives for Newlyn. By this time she evidently found beauty in the sights and sounds of the village, her opinion no doubt softened by her years of enjoyable experience there.

Elizabeth's mother continued to live with the couple after they were married and they all shared a house that was called Cliff Castle. Despite putting aside her etching, Elizabeth pursued a range of media including pastel, oil and watercolour. She carried on with her drawing and illustration throughout

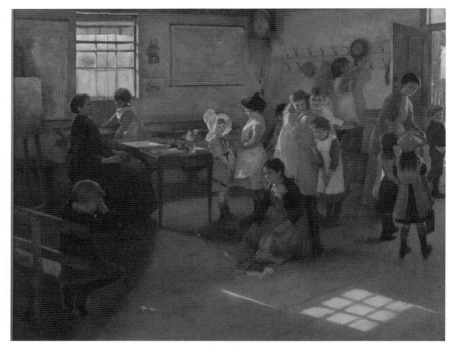

Elizabeth Adela Forbes's School is Out, *1889, oil on canvas.*

her married life. Even though her work was not exhibited in major London galleries as frequently as when she'd been single, she nevertheless continued to sell and exhibit her work widely in less illustrious galleries. During her twenty-three years of marriage she constantly worked and even after she gave birth to her son on 26 May 1893, she was not deterred from her work.

Elizabeth was remembered for sitting in fields and gardens in her little wooden moveable shelter. She set up a little temporary studio and was able to paint out of doors in most weather conditions. Her husband remembers these temporary studios, as if he was walking in his 'mind's eye':

> We have still to climb that terrible hill that leads up into the higher land above to see the favourite haunts of our landscape painters. Wandering inland we may perhaps be overtaken by some of them spinning past, with canvas and brushes strapped to their bicycles, hurrying to their daily task; perhaps out on the moors, or in the heart of some quiet wood, catch the sight of those little wooden shanties, excellent movable studios, which some have adopted lately.

Newlyn School of Art, now Newlyn Art Gallery, 2007.

It was these studies in the fields, and tireless observation, that enabled her to capture the Cornish countryside so expertly. When she died, at the age of 52, she was in her prime and her last works did not lose any of their quality of life.

Rail Links 'Up Country'
The railway and Tamar bridge opened up the region to tourists in greater numbers and facilitated easier visits both to and from Cornwall. A guidebook for such visitors was written in 1895, entitled *Clarks Guide Book of Cornwall*. It describes Newlyn and the artist colony:

Newlyn is a large fishing village, almost a suburb of Penzance, best known to the outer world by the works of the so-called 'Newlyn School' of artists, who here form a sociable colony, and keep up a dramatic club, sometimes giving public performances for charitable purposes. The main feature of this school is a Belgian or Parisian treatment. Among the best-known members are Mr and Mrs Stanhope Forbes, Messrs Bramley, Craft, Langley, Garstin, Gotch and Chevalier Taylor. A permanent gallery is being established thanks to Mr Passmore Edwards, whose name turns up in Cornwall as often as Tregeale's.

The railway also meant it was not too difficult to go to London should Forbes wish to. However, he had a distinct dislike for city life. He was aware of the strong argument to spend time in London but dreaded such visits. He bemoaned the fact that he was always being strongly advised to go to the capital, presumably to mix with his contemporaries and with those influential in the art scene of the day. He was of the mind that it was unnecessary. He found a happy solution in the cluster of artists who had congregated in that small corner of the Duchy and it suited him to live a quiet life in a more rural district with his close companions associated with the Newlyn School.

In later years Forbes's unswerving insistence to remain 'cut off' from the rest of the art world, especially in London, may well have been to the detriment of his work. There is no doubt Forbes created his best work in the 1880s and he struggled to find the same level of success from then on. His resolute rigidity to his standards of hard work and draftsmanship was in some ways preventing him from exploring other styles. He refused to consider forms of modern art at the turn of the twentieth century with their unusual colours, spontaneity and subsequent freedom from academic strictures.

Despite this he never tired of painting the beloved corner of Cornwall that he made his own. In 1893 Stanhope and Elizabeth Forbes had moved to the top of Paul Hill, to Trewarveneth Farm, which gave them more scope for painting pastoral scenes inland. *The New Calf*, painted in 1896, and *Across The Stream*, a year later, were his responses to rural Cornish life. Elizabeth's most notable work at this time, just before her death, was *Blackberry Gatherers*. Not only is it evocative of a West Penwith rural landscape but the woman and two girls picking fruit are brought alive with exuberant colour in broad, fluid brush strokes.

It is interesting to note that after the death of his wife in 1912 and the death of their only son in the First World War, Forbes's work became increasingly less focused on people. This is entirely conjecture, but it is almost as if he lost the heart to draw so close to others, or maybe could no longer cope with the intimacy of human contact. From that time onwards he began to paint street scenes in Penzance, Penryn and Helston, and although people were part of the general scene, they were no longer the central focus. The results were accurate architectural pieces and views across a town. Similarly, his later portrayals of the Cornish countryside portray distant characters who are of secondary importance to the landscape and lack the early characterisation that he considered to have been imperative.

In many ways Forbes's final years have a sense of melancholy and isolation. Many of the original artists had left Cornwall unable to find their niche with such strong competition in one locality. He and his wife had been an extraordinary team and the loss of his family would have left him bereft. He did marry again but his teaching work appears to have dwindled with the Newlyn School losing the dynamism it once had. The classes seem to have gradually been phased out and continued in a less prominent way.

The art scene no longer acknowledged Forbes's work with such favour, because tastes had changed and other styles caught the interest of the critics. Yet despite all this he appears to have derived much comfort from the countryside, as he never tired of immersing himself in nature. He constantly painted out of doors and never wearied of the open air. It is perhaps apt to close with one of his more optimistic quotes when his wife was still alive. The 'sketch' to which he refers is the description he penned in the magazine's article:

> We have at times been charged with a tendency to a grey and sombre tone, to a love of gloomy and depressing motives. I am glad that this sketch of mine, this little picture of Newlyn life, cannot incur such censure, for it shows a singularly happy and fortunate community, and the sun which we are told is wanting in our pictures has not failed to shine upon our lives.

CHAPTER 6

TRANSPORT

Cornwall has a dispersed population, so today is significantly reliant on private car ownership. Although there is adequate public transport, it is not as frequent as in cities elsewhere. Added to this, the influx of seasonal visitors, thanks to the opening of the Tamar bridge in 1961, means that many of the roads periodically suffer from excessive congestion.

It wasn't until after the Second World War that the motorcar became commonplace, although several were known to have ventured down in the 1920s. Motoring today, for the majority, is a necessary 'evil' that allows them to travel from one place to the next. We avoid traffic congestion at all costs and have lost touch with the sheer pleasure of tootling along for fun, perfectly happily at 20 miles per hour.

Saltash ferry and bridge, Plymouth, in 1959 as it was before the Tamar bridge was built. The ferry was the only means of travelling in a motorcar to Cornwall.

The Tamar bridge, Saltash, being constructed prior to its opening in 1961.

It is a Cornishman who we have to thank (and possibly sometimes begrudge) for many advances in the motorcar. Donald M. Healey CBE, born in Perranporth in 1898, was the designer of the Austin Healey.

There is something distinctly stylish about the classic cars he designed; the air of gentility seems to encapsulate the elegance and motoring finesse of a bygone era. Healey was known to take great care with the many aesthetic details inside his vehicles; the leather upholstery, convex domed chrome side-mirrors, cigar lighter and switches that pleasingly 'clunk' on or off.

Bodinnick motor ferry for Polperro and Looe in 1930.

Falmouth Hotel and Cliff Road in 1905, four miles from Healey's family home, as it was before the motorcar started to visit in great numbers.

By taking down the canvas hood, motorists would have been able to experience the countryside with all their senses, something from which today's high-tech vehicles insulate us.

After tinkering in his youth with all things mechanical, Healey went on to be a successful English rally driver winning the Monte Carlo Rally in 1931. He was, however, perhaps best known for being a designer and engineer with the British Motor Corporation. He died in 1988.

Enthusiasts continue to travel down to regularly relive a snapshot of history by driving, as Healey would have done, in a classic car along the

After the road was built in 1907.

A boating lake in West Looe, 1935.
By necessity it has been turned into a car park.

winding Cornish lanes. Without road markings and streetlights it is possible to imagine yourself back in time before these halcyon days of pleasure driving were lost to us.

Trebah House and Garden was his marital home before being sold and transformed into a public garden. A memorial is situated there in honour of his various engineering achievements.

Nowadays we have come to despise traffic's pollutant properties, but we may still find much enjoyment in driving, even though we are aware it comes at a cost to the environment. This is something Healey and his early fellow motorists would not have fully appreciated. The days of motoring exclusively as an infrequent luxury and pleasure have been lost; today driving has become routine. Likewise, the time when we could allow children to freely play on the roads and allow herds of pigs to meander through a village have gone for good.

Sea Trading

Before the railways were built Cornish industrial trading relied predominantly on seagoing transportation. In other industrial areas of Britain canals were built to overcome transport difficulties but because water trafficking had been commonplace in Cornwall for centuries, the majority of bulk cargo was transported by sea. There are more than thirty ports along the Cornish coast. Ships either made their way around the coastline, mostly heading for

*Charlestown, St Austell, in 1903 when sailing ships were
at the height of their glory.*

London, or taking to the high seas and traversing international waters to the
rest of the British colonies and merchant allies.

Roads in Cornwall until the late 1800s were notoriously impassable and
little more than mud tracks, so carts and carriages were rarely employed.
However, small coves, creeks, and the many rivers in the region meant that
small boats were by far the easiest way of moving from place to place. There
were many quays along the Rivers Tamar, Truro, Fowey and Fal that were
suitable for small passenger vessels. Passengers with local business concerns
and lighter consignments of goods were taken by barge, cock boat or ferry
boat across rivers and estuaries.

Many of Cornwall's tidal estuaries are still crossed by ferries as they
were in the past. Nowadays many operate during the summer season only
and are no longer essential for daily transport. Ferries around the Carrick
Roads, the Fal, the Fowey, the Camel and the Helford Passage provide passenger services for day excursions and recreational purposes, which are
hardly indicative of their once-crucial status. But the traveller only has to
take a trip, just twenty-six miles off Land's End to the Scilly Isles, and there
is a genuine, daily, working need for ferry boats. Islanders continue to rely
on sea transport for almost every provision and excursion. By spending
time on the islands it is possible to imagine how it must have been elsewhere in Cornwall before road and rail travel and before the daily use of
ferries declined. Barges, cutters, luggers, sloops, brigantines, yachts and

Newquay's North Quay, which has since been washed away, as it was in 1887.

barks were all types of boat used for different purposes, all functioning tools of the seafaring community. Even the boats whose main purpose or function was fishing would have been used to transport provisions and passengers as the need arose.

Probably the most notable of all seagoing craft were the famous Falmouth packet ships operating out of Falmouth harbour between the years 1688 and 1852. Packets were small brigantines, which were designed to achieve higher speeds than larger ships. The Post Office appointed Falmouth as its central location for an international mail service when it was no more than a large village. The packet ships were 'Crown ships' and sailed regularly from 1702 to Barbados, Jamaica and the Southern States of North America. Two years later a Lisbon service was established. By 1706 regular trips were made to the West Indies, Nova Scotia, Mexico, Brazil and Argentina.

Prior to this, mail was carried in a far less regular way by naval or merchant ships and usually only if they had space on board or were available to make the voyage. By 1827 approximately forty packets were operating regularly from Falmouth. Mail was parcelled up in leather-bound bags treated with plenty of beeswax to protect against the ocean spray. The open end was either stitched with thick thread or stapled using metal rivets to aid security. Should the safety of a packet fall under threat the crew had strict instructions to sink the mail rather than let it fall into enemy hands. They also carried bullion and provided a vital commercial link between Britain, the colonies and other overseas destinations.

The Regatta at Saltash in 1927 – a celebration of small seafaring craft.

In Arthur Norway's *History of the Post-Office Packet Service* written in 1895 he bewails the loss of these splendid vessels:

> But there remains a service distinguished over and over again, an ancient service, highly useful to the public, and associated with a great department of state, whose history has been left untold till all the offices connected with it have passed away and the personal recollections which are the life-blood of such a narrative are lost to us irretrievably – I refer to the Post-Office Packet Service.

There is indeed scant information to draw upon save the official documents that list various administrative changes. However, Norway's book is a wealth of anecdotal information, with snippets that can be pieced together to form a more comprehensive overview, allowing greater insight into the history of Falmouth's packets.

Today, thanks to some in-depth research (several publications and the work of the National Maritime Museum), more is known about these valiant small ships. But there is still widespread unfamiliarity with the history of packet ships and, indeed, how crucial they were in safeguarding the British Isles. Even in the generation after they stopped operating, Norway suggests that their significance was lost:

> The very name has grown unfamiliar to our ears. It brings nothing

to our minds, recalls no train of recollections, stirs up no dim memories. For the whole world, with the exception of a few people in Cornwall and on the east coast of England, the Packet service is dead, like all the men who made it, and fought in it, and laid their lives down for it.

These glorious constructions of rigging and sail were notoriously dangerous to voyage within and were infamously dubbed 'coffin ships' by the locals. Yet it was not the sea storms presenting such peril but, rather, hostile action from other foreign ships during the French Revolutionary and Napoleonic Wars.

There was many an anxious loved one who waited eagerly for the return of their man or boy who had set off several weeks earlier on a voyage. A watchman was appointed to keep vigil on the top of Beacon Hill above Falmouth port. The instant a packet came into view he would rush into the town to spread the news. Boats manned by a team of sturdy rowers would set out from the inner harbour to meet the packet and assist the crew ashore, ensuring safe docking for all concerned.

The people of Falmouth who waited on the quayside knew only too well that these crews faced danger of all kinds from pirates and privateers (privately owned ships employed by governments to seize and plunder enemy vessels during wartime). Some of these damaged ships would return to Falmouth with their hulls bearing the signs of gunshot, and timbers blackened by fires lit by arsonists. A few survivors might have sailed their battered vessel home with the telltale signal of an ensign (flag of nation) at half-mast in honour of those who had been killed by hostile hands. It was only thanks to swift and expert seamanship that these ships were able to get away with sufficient speed to survive these attacks.

After 1703 there was a relief fund for those who returned wounded, which could be administered by the packet's agent to grant compensation. Recompense could be made for amputated limbs, and varying degrees of loss of sight.

There were terrifying tales of Algerian pirates capturing a crew because so many of the packets were ill armed and unable to retaliate. Countless seafaring men were subjected to sale into white slavery; some later made it back to Cornish soil to tell their story. Many were not so fortunate and faced the worst possible kinds of deaths, or were known to endure immeasurable misery under slave labour in North Africa or elsewhere.

However, the Falmouth men were known to have carried out a little piracy of their own, as Norway's 1895 account states:

But it is certain that a good deal of piracy in a quiet way was done by Falmouth commanders, especially early in the century, when the control from headquarters was lax, and the necessity of watching the use made of the armaments supplied by the Government was not clearly seen. The officers showed a disposition to call the irregularity 'privateering'; but a vessel that takes prizes without a license from the Crown is a pirate, not a Privateer, and the packets never held such licenses.

Packet crews traded their own supplies of cigars, port wine, and brandy, transferring the prized cargo into sloops and brigs and smuggling it ashore at night. Many of these activities may have benefited the officers and their men but they were strongly condemned by the Postmaster General whose primary concern was the safety of the mail. Despite the punishment of offenders this activity clearly continued, it being one of the main reasons known for not arming the packets too heavily. The guards might report any illegalities to the Crown. Increased weaponry and armed guards came to be provided on the packets by 1837 because the Empire's security was under increased threat, and merchants and the military were by then relying so heavily on the vessels for communication.

The concept of regular packet boats was not entirely novel, as similar services ran up England's east coast by Dover and Harwich. Falmouth was nevertheless considered by the government to be the most suitable harbour in the British Isles. This was mainly due to the advantages of its vast, natural, deep-water bay, facilitating the passage of ships without tidal restrictions. For centuries merchant and naval ships had benefited from its sheltered aspect, which protected it from the worst of the Atlantic storms. Vessels could normally begin a voyage in all weathers confident that, for the start of the journey at least, they could establish a working rhythm. They were able to avoid collision with other vessels in the harbour's uniquely safe waters known to allow more manageable manoeuvring. Norway concurs with the Royal Mail's decision to use Falmouth:

The right port was chosen there cannot be a doubt. The extreme westerly position of Falmouth Harbour gives it an advantage, which is rendered evident by a single glance at a map. From no other harbour in this country can an outward-bound vessel clear the land so soon. No other is so quickly reached by one homeward bound running for shelter. On the darkest nights and in dense fog, ships acquainted with the harbour enter it in safety, so easy is it to access, and sailing vessels can leave in any wind, save one blowing strongly from the east or south east. The prevalent gales in the English Channel are from the West. These are head winds for a ship leaving Plymouth, the port with which Falmouth is most naturally compared; but they are favourable for Falmouth.

Life on board offered the officers, men, and paying passengers the very worst kind of living conditions. Their quarters were damp and cramped, and life below deck was without natural light or decent ventilation. Some of the hatches could be opened in fine weather but when it rained there was no fresh air.

Rats were a persistent hazard, not simply due to the health concerns they presented, but they were a genuine menace to safety. They could gnaw through essential ropes, or even a ship's timbers causing serious leaks.

The majority of the crew slept in hammocks slung between the ship's beams. They were allowed a small box in which to keep their personal effects. There were no toilet facilities, save the 'bucket and chuck it' method and little privacy of any kind. Paying passengers on the cheapest passages endured similar conditions. On the other hand, wealthier gentlemen, traders, diplomats, merchants and their families were given separate quarters, sleeping in wooden bunks.

Food consisted of portions of salted beef or pork, including trotters, snouts (with accompanying nose rings), and skin complete with hairs. This was all endured on a limited ration of water. Biscuits and dried peas were included in the supplies but any kind of liquor was prohibited while travelling on a packet ship by order of the Crown.

All food was prepared centrally in a large copper cauldron and cooks struggled to keep their fires alight against the onslaught of sea spray. Pease soup was available as a regular staple meal.

It must have been an absolute boon when techniques to distill sea water were mastered and drinking water was no longer such a rarity, especially in hotter climates, when a passenger suffered seasickness, or was forced to spend long hours in a poorly ventilated cabin below deck suffering from fever. It is a wonder anybody survived these overwhelming hardships.

Post Office packets were the nearest thing to a modern news agency. The officers on board had strict instructions to detail every event of public importance in their ship's journal. These accounts provided the most accurate and authentic news from overseas. As soon as a packet arrived, and the journal was taken to the Post Office for inspection, a crowd of merchants would be waiting for news of any political or commercial significance to their interests.

The packets brought a great deal of prosperity to Falmouth and the Post Office service grew steadily stronger by the end of the eighteenth century. The town grew and developed as a consequence and the State Department was established in the midst of it. Some 1,200 men were employed by the Post Office and up to 3,000 paying passengers took voyages on the packets each year.

As the number of packets increased, local tradesmen prospered. Naval supplies were needed incessantly and there were constant demands on all kinds of local supplies. Shipbuilding yards sprang up, ropewalks were laid out for ease of boarding and inns built for the accommodation of travellers.

Don Manuel Alvarez Espriella (Robert Southey's *nom de plume*), a traveller, left an account of the town in his published letters of 1808, which Norway transcribes within his publication. It provides a humorous and vivid account of a Falmouth inn at the height of the packet service in 1802:

> The perpetual stir and bustle in this inn is as surprising as it is wearisome. Doors opening and shutting, bells ringing, voices calling to the waiter from every quarter, while he cries, 'coming' to one room and hurries away to another. Everybody is in a hurry here, either they are going off to the Packets and are hastening their preparations to embark, or they have just arrived and are impatient to be on the road homeward. Every now and then a carriage rattles up to the door with a rapidity which makes the very house shake. The man who cleans the boots is running in one direction, the barber with his powder bag in another. There goes the barber's boy with his hot water and razors; there comes the clean linen from the washerwoman, and the hall is full of porters and sailors bringing up luggage, or bearing it away. Now you hear a horn blow because the post is coming in, and in the middle of the night you are awakened by another because it is going out. Nothing is done in England without a noise, and yet noise is the only thing they forget in the bill.

Steamers made tentative challenges to the packets' trafficking monopoly. These attempts at long voyages were experimental at first, with spectacular failures as steamers ran out of essential fuel. This necessitated their being towed back into harbour by sailing vessels. One can imagine the scathing

Millbrook Steamers in 1907 when steamships began to become more popular throughout Cornwall.

derogatory remarks made at the sight of their plight.

The packets' glory days were relatively short-lived because, increasingly, ships were relocated to other ports. Several steamships took over the mail service to destinations such as Greece, Malta, Portugal and the West Indies. By 1850 the majority of packet ships were no longer required in Falmouth and the service was mostly transferred to Southampton. A significant chapter of Cornish maritime history was brought to a close.

Over Land
Myriad tracks and footpaths cross Cornwall's peninsula, linking towns with villages and scattered farms. An intricate network of byways and bridleways were, at one time, the primary thoroughfares when the majority of local journeys were made by foot. Ancient ridge-ways crossed high moorland in more remote areas so that travel was restricted to foot or horseback. Many of these tracks were no more than gullies with loose rocks and stones, and large boulders embedded like steps to negotiate along the way.

Now they are mostly used for recreation, but in the 1700s and early 1800s they were vital for sustaining communication, and trade across land, although this was mostly for domestic and parochial needs, most business conducted with more distant places was carried out by sea.

The lack of predictable road surfaces made any journey arduous. Cornwall's poor roads, many winding up and down remarkably steep hills with stony, rutted surfaces no doubt reinforced its sense of remoteness. Mules and cob horses were commonly used, as they were less liable to fall prey to injury, unlike finer thoroughbreds, and made for a sturdier ride across potholes and uneven ground. Ingenious methods of strapping goods to the animals' backs were devised, with a packsaddle made of leather or canvas, yoke or, in some cases, a wooden sledge towed behind. Lanes were and still are narrow, winding and liable to flood if the drainage was not considered and maintained. Even mules were unable to negotiate through some poorly repaired lanes, especially if there had been a heavy downpour or persistent rain had turned the ground into a quagmire.

The early 1800s relied upon thousands of packhorses and mules for all industrial goods. They were the main link between ports, quarries, mines, market-places and farms. These animals were an essential part of the industrial prosperity of Cornwall and around the busier ports, such as at Hayle and Portreath, hundreds, if not thousands of loads were transported each day to and from the quays. There was an extensive network of carriers whose main purpose was to transport goods and supply cargo to the ports and waterborne transport. This all required immense effort and was a labourious process, loading and unloading one saddle's burden at a time.

Attempts were made to improve matters although progress was slow in creating better highways. Turnpike roads were developed as a means of raising a level of responsibility amongst parish officials for stretches of the highway in their jurisdiction. Turnpikes were set up in Launceston, Liskeard, Lostwithiel, Callington, Bodmin, St Austell, Tregony and other towns.

Tollgates were introduced and fees levied by trusts, whose role it was to maintain the road in its care. Revenues raised from these fees were used to fund the work of improving a turnpike route. In some cases roads were improved considerably for ease of travelling, with granite hardcore and cobbles being individually laid by hand. In other areas the situation was not so favourable, with only the basic infilling of the deepest ruts with rubble, and half-hearted clearing of some ditches for drainage. By far the best road surface was created by breaking up and crushing lumps of rock with lump hammers, the gritty surface being packed down hard. This made a durable, safer and smoother surface. But this method was costly in time and manpower, so tended to be used on the essential mail and bullion routes that were concentrated around higher population centres and important ports.

In 1798, the well-known road engineer, John Louden McAdam, settled in Falmouth. It was through his initiative, particularly, that fresh impetus was given to attend to road systems. It became considered vital by influential merchants and landowners that improved routes over land were a helpful way of bringing prosperity to the region.

Although, in principle, English laws were supposed to bear upon trusts that were remiss, there seemed to have been some disparity between theory and practice. An ad-hoc system existed to monitor the quality of works carried out and there was no central controlling authority.

Herds of cattle and pigs, on the way to market or watering holes, were liable to churn up unmade surfaces with their hooves. In some areas tolls were charged per score, which tended to persuade herdsmen to choose other more isolated routes instead. Pedestrians paid no toll at all.

There are tollhouses in most towns whose occupants in the eighteenth and nineteenth centuries were assigned to collect money from all vehicular travellers, apart from passing mail coaches. By the 1620s post could be sent using the government system of organised horseback riders connecting with water-based vessels called postal barques.

A toll house on the road to St Just, near Lands End, is situated on a cross-roads with windows overlooking all approaches.

Tollkeepers (pikemen) were provided with a home, being on call twenty-four hours a day and needing to be available to lift the toll barriers and collect the fee. Close to a byway, bridge or crossroads these pikemen were entrusted with the job of controlling all traffic, being on watch for all approaching travellers.

The first or last tollhouse of the land is situated on the St Just road from Penzance in the parish of Sancreed and is now a private residence in a prominent position on this busy road. Such buildings often tended to have a distinct octagonal architectural style that is easily discernable to the informed eye, although in some areas they are varied in design. Because of the official nature of these buildings they were sometimes reflective of military designs or gatehouses from larger estates. Some had gothic-style windows offering panoramic views to all road directions. Most houses were built of granite, under slate roofs and had a door and porch facing the road. A board with toll charges was displayed outside.

The first Cornish tollhouses are likely to have been located along roads entering Cornwall in the mid-1700s. A specific single-storey design seems to have been adopted and used in other areas too. With a design including a scullery, privy and a distinct bay at the main front entrance, these homes were modest in size.

All Cornish tollhouses are now under private ownership and their original use obsolete, yet at one time every traveller would have been mindful of their need to pay at the turnpike barrier.

Cornish Coaching

Elizabeth I was among the first to experience travelling in the spring-less hollow turning coach and was not particularly enamoured. However, this early horse-drawn coach gradually came into use on State occasions and the nobility started to favour this mode of transport. But it was not until 1634 that the first London coaches were hired for public use.

The first coach owned in Cornwall belonged to the Hawkins family in St Erth in the early 1700s, being donated to the Royal Cornwall Museum in Truro in the early 1900s. In the late 1700s there were several chaises used in Falmouth and up until this time wheeled transport in Cornwall was a rarity. These carriages were seen throughout the principal Cornish towns thereafter, especially after the turnpike routes made travelling by road less hazardous.

In the late 1700s the first stagecoach ran regularly between Exeter and Falmouth via Bodmin, this being the initial establishment of more regular public coach services.

Far from being comfortable these vehicles were renowned for giving rough and jolting journeys along unbearably difficult roads. Winter travel was especially trying for passengers and even more so for those who paid for a cheaper seat on top of the coach, out in the elements where hypothermia was a very real threat.

In the late 1800s it took nearly a week to travel to London on a stage-coach from Cornwall. The arduous journey was uncertain and fraught with many kinds of mishaps and difficulties. It is therefore not surprising that many families preferred to sail to Bristol or Portsmouth in preference to the more expensive chaise services.

Mail Coaches

Since earliest times any kind of message was carried by a young boy or a man by foot or on horseback for a fee. These services were only as reliable as the individual entrusted with the errand and there are infamous accounts of vital communication links disintegrating simply due to dawdling or drunkenness. So when the new stagecoach was introduced it was welcomed for its speed and the facility of mailbag drops at the stage-post inns.

When the Cornishman, Edmund Prideaux, first established the Post Office in 1644, a postal system was introduced to convey letters between Exeter and Launceston. Highwaymen often intercepted these coaches, the post being lost.

The travelling horse-drawn fair on Penzance quay in 1895.

Fore Street and the Town Hall in East Looe in 1905 when horse and cart or carriage was the main form of transport overland.

It was John Palmer from Bath who introduced the safer mail coach to run between Bristol and London. There are few records of mail coaches running in Cornwall until the late 1700s and even then, the old method of carriage 'by foot' continued for the majority of deliveries. Palmer's idea was to employ special safer, faster, privately owned coaches instead of the old stagecoaches, with a guard to guarantee the safe delivery of mail. These coaches also took a few paying travellers and were an instant success because of the much-improved service.

Granite signposts can still be found along many roads in Cornwall today, with mileage and destination inscribed as a lasting testimony to these well-trodden routes. Inns acted as post-stages where travellers would rest overnight, eat a meal or hire horses. Mail could be delivered and kept safe for the intended recipient.

Regular horse changes took place through Cornwall near St Austell, Perranwharf, Truro, Ladcock, Indian Queens, Goss Moor, Roche, Bodmin, Bodmin Moor and Launceston.

Torpoint's steam ferry in the mid-to-late 1800s, known as the 'floating bridge', made for an even speedier journey from Plymouth across to Cornwall and the entire carriage with harnessed horses could be taken across the river without much difficulty.

The most significant role of the Cornish mail coaches was to carry the Falmouth packets off the packet ships. These government dispatches, arriving from all over the globe, were accompanied by armed guards.

Roads were greatly improved in Cornwall between 1820 and 1849 due to the prosperity of the mining industry and other trades.

Although horse-drawn coaches are a rarity today the coaching inns of old survive. Once, the main functions of these prominent hostelries was to provide rest and refreshment for weary travellers from the stage and mail coaches passing through. It was in the stables that horses were changed over, mail offloaded for local destinations and passengers were able to rest for a short while or overnight.

The most significant coaching inns in Cornwall were Town Arms Hotel, Jewel's Hotel and Oliver's Royal Hotel in Bodmin, Wellington Hotel in Boscastle, Falcon Hotel and Carriers' Inn in Bude, Golding's Hotel in Callington, Mathews' Hotel in Camborne, The Kings Arms in Camelford, Halfway House in Drawbridge, Royal Hotel, King's Arms, Duke's Head Hotel and Green Bank Hotel in Falmouth, Queen's Head in Grampound, White Hart in Hayle, Star Inn and The Angel in Helston.

The guards on a stage and mail coach sounded a brass horn to announce their approach to an inn or tollgate. Some played bugle simply to entertain themselves and their fare-paying customers on the long journeys. At some point, bugles were officially banned, a single horn blast being used instead. One can only imagine there were numerous complaints presented by customers!

The last mail coaches ran in 1919 from Bude and this system of transport came to a close after more than 120 years. The age of the railway had begun.

By Rail

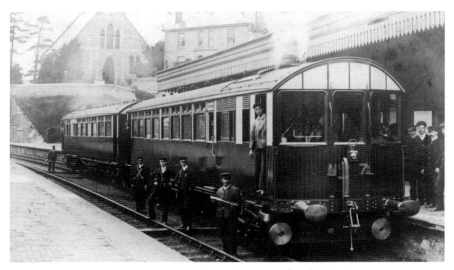

A train waiting in the station at Saltash in 1906.

The development of rail links in Cornwall can be singularly attributed to one man's influence, Isambard Kingdom Brunel. As an engineer with the Great Western Railway, Cornwall and West Cornwall Companies, he commanded oversight of the line between Paddington and Penzance. GWR purchased the West Cornwall Railway, the Cornwall Railway and the Minerals Railway and extended its own lines to St Ives and Bodmin, followed by Liskeard and Caradon, and the Liskeard and Looe branch lines. Construction of the line between Plymouth and Falmouth began in about 1852. The Hayle route to Redruth already existed, although the line needed to be replaced after much use by local mines and foundries, having operated from 1837. This line was extended to form the West Cornwall Railway from Penzance to Truro in 1852. The Cornwall line contains an extraordinary number of viaducts, thirty-four in total, along the Plymouth to Truro line.

Brunel's Royal Albert Bridge, completed in 1859, opened up Cornwall

St Germans viaduct in 1906. It still takes the main line train through
Cornwall but there is no longer a platform at St Germans.

to the rest of mainland Britain. Over 640 metres in length and 30 metres in height, it stretched across the River Tamar, a spectacular feat of engineering in iron. Prince Albert, after whom the bridge was named, attended as guest of honour at the opening ceremony where he was greeted by cheering crowds and brass bands.

Thomas Harvey, a somewhat lesser-known personality with a dogged determination in the face of continual opposition, strove to implement his personal vision for a central Cornish rail line. His contemporaries stood against him as he initially fought alone for the pioneering power of steam to make its way from Falmouth through the Cornish moors to Saltash. The tin mines and quarries were already using their own railway lines but Harvey was proposing a new commercial freight and passenger service.

Edward Osler in his *History of the Cornwall Railway 1835–1846* takes an extract from the *Cornwall Gazette* and reprinted it in 1846. His quote highlights how the majority closed their ears to the voice of progress. Those present at the meeting showed concern that the railway could take essential transportation trade away from Falmouth, depriving Cornwall's shipping of its advantages:

> The project originated with Mr. Thomas Harvey, a solicitor then of
> Falmouth, who attended the meeting at Truro in January 1844 at
> which the Cornwall Railway was formed, and there contended at

*The rail line at Perranporth in 1911 when it was in regular use. Now the
nearest station is Truro and the town's old station is a private house.*

considerable length for a line to be carried direct over the moors to
Exeter, supporting his views by quotations from a report by Capt.
Moorson. He was not suffered to finish his speech, for the meeting
interfered and stopped him, and none supported his views. Not discouraged by this, he put himself in communication with the officers
of the South west railway.

Harvey promoted the formation of a central line through Cornwall from
Exeter. The extent to which the rail links to Plymouth and beyond transformed the livelihoods of the Cornish cannot be overestimated. As was
mentioned in previous chapters, the convenience to fishermen, farmers and
other industries and trades was phenomenal.

Other railway stations were opened into the 1900s, including Chacewater,
Newquay, St Agnes, Perranporth, Bodmin, Wadebridge, Padstow, Camelford,
Launceston, and various smaller stops were established as the railway became
more popular.

It could be argued that the most significant train service contributing to
Cornwall's prosperity was GWR's Cornish Rivieria, originally named The
Cornish Rivieria Limited. This was at a time when the mining industry was
in decline. The express steam locomotive travelling between Paddington and
Penzance was advertised to attract visitors from outside the region. In the

early 1900s, iconic posters were printed to suggest that Cornwall's climate was comparable to that of southern Europe. We know that Cornwall is certainly a milder place than most in the British Isles, but it is far from sunny all year round. The service did, however, open up the tourist trade, making Cornwall a favourite seaside holiday destination.

GWR's Cornish Rivieria first ran on 1 July 1904, taking just seven hours from Paddington to Penzance. Initially the carriages were pulled by Churchward 'Star' class engines until, in the 1920s, they were replaced by the Collett 'Castles' and 'Kings'. The 'bulldog' engine, with its smaller wheels, hauled the luxurious coaches west of Plymouth.

There still remains a great affection for these majestic, historic locomotives, substituted by diesel engines in 1957. Some of the great, former engines have been lovingly preserved and emerge from storage on special occasions. Unfortunately, most were scrapped, many branch lines having been taken up. For those who want to experience this great piece of Cornish heritage, all is not completely lost; the Bodmin and Wenford Railway remains in operation. It is possible to imagine, for a few brief moments, that you have stepped back in time. Yet there is something not entirely genuine in this tourist attraction. It offers a simulated experience, dedicated to enjoyment rather than the service of everyday life. You will not find crates of live hens on their way to market, or freshly picked purple sprouting broccoli off to Covent Garden, London.

In reality, original tracks have been lifted, being left as overgrown paths, desolation having descended around obsolete platforms.

Electric Tramcars

In addition to mineral traffic, a new electric tram system was introduced in 1902, between the towns of Redruth and Camborne, taking in the smaller towns and villages of Illogan Highway, Pool and Tuckingmill. The service catered for the thousands of miners and their families in the area, along with all associated trades people that needed to work between the two main towns.

Operating seven days a week, the tram service enabled local residents greater ease of movement, being especially popular in wet weather.

Throughout the two world wars a service continued to be maintained despite the general depression affecting the region's economy, although the service was reduced.

In 1925, the Motor Transport Company started to run single-deck buses, taking on the same routes as the trams. After a couple of spectacular failures to provide a tram service following electrical storms, buses rescued the

The electric tram in Trelowarren Street, Camborne, in 1905,
which ran to and from Redruth.

stranded passengers. The tramway finally closed in 1927 after twenty-five years of continuous operation. Bus transport increasingly displaced the old trams. Tracks and overhead power supply cables were removed.

Camborne and Redruth Mineral Line in 1930 at the junction
east of Pool, looking east.

Pilot Gigs

These zippy six-oared rowing boats are far from lost to us thanks to the dedication and determination of a few enthusiasts. There was a time in the 1900s when gigs were laid up, burned, or left to rot following the introduction of the motorboat. Once the historic significance of the pilot gig was recognised, a salvage and restoration process took place, and some of the oldest rowing boats in Britain were painstakingly brought back into operation.

Now these extraordinary boats are mostly used for sport and pleasure, where in times past they were essentially used as working boats. The initial date that gigs were used throughout every coastal town in Cornwall is often debated, but the eighteenth and nineteenth centuries saw their main use.

The gig's primary purpose was to transport pilots to incoming ships as they prepared to dock. The pilot was a master mariner whose role was to take over the manoeuvring of a vessel through shallow water. He was familiar with the many dangers, having an in-depth knowledge of local waters, rocks and tides. Without his help a ship could be left to tragically flounder in potentially treacherous seas.

The pilot gig consisted of six stalwart rowers and a coxswain who were prepared to venture into open seas whatever the time of day or prevailing weather conditions. The gig was crafted for speed and sea-keeping qualities but needed carrying capacity too.

The most notable longstanding gig-building family, were the Peters of Polvarth, St Mawes. William Peters founded his boat shed in 1793, and after him followed three more generations of Peters: William his son, then John and finally Nicholas. Several of their original gigs have been lovingly preserved.

Made from Cornish small-leafed elm, these gigs are a standard 32 feet long with a beam of 4 feet 10 inches. The Peters family had a ready supply of timber in the woodlands around the Fal and Roseland Peninsula. The original oars were made from felled ash, being 18 feet long, but the design for today's racing paddle is far shorter.

The most significant builder of gigs today is Ralph Bird who works out of Devoran, having learned his craft and techniques from the Peters family.

Not only were these rowing boats used to transport pilots, but they were also an invaluable resource as early inshore lifeboats. Because gig crews were experienced in the most taxing of conditions at sea, their ability to cope in a crisis was invaluable to a ship's crew in difficulty. Numerous are the stories of rescue, especially around the Isles of Scilly, as these fearless rowers mastered the waves and tides to bring grateful survivors ashore.

SS Tripolitania *wrecked on Looe Bar on Boxing Day in December 1912.*

In Captain J.N. Taylor's *Plans of Harbours, Rivers and Sea Ports*, he writes in 1840 extensively about the Isles of Scilly, giving detailed information on the approach from open seas. He cites various hazardous rocky outcrops, unusual tides and states:

> ...it has two channels; one is called the Northwest Channel, the other the Southwest channel... each of them is dangerous to those who are not well acquainted with the marks and settings of the tides.

The rescued crew of SS Tripolitania *circa 27 December 1912.*

Gig crews appointed a lookout to watch the ocean twenty-four hours a day. The crew urgently raced towards any approaching ship because the first boat to arrive was rewarded with the contract to guide it into port. The famous competitive, racing spirit was born from such intense team rivalry.

The pilot of the first gig was thrown a rope ladder to climb aboard. He took control of the vessel, guiding her through narrow and rocky waters to safe anchorage.

At other times gigs were employed to carry passengers and freight, being especially useful for salvaging a wreck. These were the predecessors of more recent lifeboat crews, wrecks being commonplace around the Cornish coast during the seventeenth and eighteenth centuries. These valiant rowers were regularly in demand. Thousands of wrecks are recorded, although not all were known of as many disappeared, lost in the night.

Many Cornish families took advantage of the floundering wrecks and the items washed ashore. Children were clothed and houses furnished in this way. All manner of goods were retrieved from cargo holds – food, timber, soap, leather, cloth, stone and metal goods.

Occasionally a gig would be rigged with a dipping lugsail and mizzen. Although they were fairly nimble under sail, gigs were essentially designed for speed rowing.

There are today more than 100 international gig clubs. The World Pilot Gig Championships take place each year on the Isles of Scilly.

Although the original use of these plucky seagoing craft has been largely usurped by the motorboat, it is reassuring that their memory, still precious to many Cornish people, is kept very much alive.

CHAPTER 7

TRADES AND OCCUPATIONS

Building

Cornwall's distinctively old-time cottages, with their crooked beams, white-washed walls, stone inglenooks and low doors and ceilings, delight the passer-by with their rustic simplicity. The well-appointed civilised Cornish cottage of today, with its casually clean interior, contrasts greatly with the probable damp 'hovel' often described in the nineteenth century. Granite stone was freely and naturally acquired from the moors; miner-crofters built their own homes from materials close at hand.

Many cottages prior to the 1900s would have been built from salvaged rubble stone and boulders from the surrounding countryside, and mixed with mud. In Cornwall there is a strong tradition of this type of building with cob. Made from the deeper subsoil, cob is rich in clay, and after combining with

The Old Success Inn at Sennen Cove being re-thatched in 1900.

straw and horsehair it was used to build up walls layer upon layer as is still practised in Third World countries today.

Internally a thick layer of plaster was formed from clay, horse or cow hair and lime for binding the mix. This was applied and finished with a top-coat of limewash. Limekilns have now been abandoned, although dozens would have once existed along all the rivers of Cornwall. These stone kiln structures, with distinctive arch, were mostly built between the early 1700s and late 1800s. The limestone had to be imported because it was scarce in Cornwall, and as well as being used as a building material in a mortar or lime putty it was also used in agriculture as a fertilizer.

Tradesmen and craftsmen would use rudimentary cob techniques to build living quarters close to, or attached to a place of work. Land, generally laid to waste, was obtained from the owner by a lease system that was dependent on the lives of three named individuals. When the last of these three people died the ownership of the land reverted back to the original owner. There was an obvious advantage to the landowner, because acres of his land was reclaimed and cultivated at no expense to himself. It also meant that working families had homes nearby.

Surprisingly, a number of these cob cottages, farm buildings and barns have survived the centuries. They are now largely transformed into ordered delights for the tourist, complete with touches of informed taste contrived to entrance. In the past these cottages were made with functionality of purpose

Traditional cottages in Lanreath 1935.

and little consideration for the picturesque. Careful deliberation about solidity and strength were the main preoccupations for the miner or farmer in the few building hours between shifts. They were amateur architects working with their own hands, without even a plan, but erecting walls to the shape of the hand-sawn timbers.

Building regulations in 1965 introduced a policy that specified a need for verifiable 'fitness of materials', which meant it was no longer sustainable to build with cob. Unlike other building materials such as stone or cement it is almost impossible to regulate the quality of cob, so building in this way ceased completely and other building materials were substituted, such as cement, granite and brick. When regulations offered more flexibility in 1985, some original buildings that needed to be preserved or extended, were once again permitted to be built with cob. This change in policy also accommodated the more 'ecologically friendly' build. Construction with Cornish cob became a celebrated bona fide structural material once more. Even so, it is a master crafting skill and few building firms today would even contemplate using what would perhaps be considered an outdated or specialist process. So despite this skill being lost to the majority of new-builds, there are a few restoration projects continuing to require cob walls.

Doors in these cottages were made of vertical timber boards and held together by two or three ledges nailed crossways. Cornish doors were of the 'hepse' variety being divided in the middle so that the top half was left open

A typical example of an old Cornish Cob wall that has been rendered.

Mr Ead, an eighty-four-year-old thatcher, at Carminnon Cross Farm in 1942.

to let in light and the bottom closed to prevent livestock entering. Latches may have been simple wooden bolts with hand-forged iron fixings. Windows were no more than a hole in the wall and were rarely glazed until the early 1800s; until then a simple shutter sufficed. Mullioned windows, or glazed lattice was a sure indication that somebody such as a yeoman, far wealthier than an unskilled labourer, inhabited a Georgian dwelling.

A plentiful supply of building stone can be found in Cornwall and as such there has been little need for brickmaking as in other areas of Britain. Bricks have been used both in industrial buildings and as a decorative facing for granite stone but their use is relatively rare in Cornwall's historical buildings.

But after 1850 there were some brickworks, the first being the Lizard Brick & Tile Works at Church Cove. Yellow bricks for the building trade were also produced by the china clay industry and Calstock was the most significant brickmaking parish in all Cornwall.

Original cob or stone cottages would have been thatched. Thatching is the oldest and most common roofing technique in the world and all smaller buildings would have been roofed with any vegetable material in the Middle Ages until the nineteenth century in rural Cornwall. Although some fine examples remain, most notably the Quaker Meeting House at Come-to-

Good, the Veryan round houses, Mullion's Old Inn and the Red Lion pub at Mawnan Smith, many other historic buildings over the years have seen their water or wheat reed thatch replaced by slate.

A thatcher in the 1841 census was considered to be a less socially important craftsman, along with the bookbinder and tailor. Old thatched cottages are now listed and preserved, However, in the past whole villages had thatches removed and were simply rebuilt with slate. Transportation of building materials became easier once the railway opened and roads improved in the late 1800s. Slate was in ready supply in Cornwall and did not require the expense of upkeep that a thatch necessitated. It is interesting that Mawnan lost its thatcher in the ten years between 1841–51. It is probable there was not enough trade to keep his business going.

Slate is a most versatile building material: it is light, durable and above all waterproof. Flag floors, windowsills and roofs were traditionally built from it, and some fine examples of building with slate can be seen at Tintagel and Boscastle.

Quarrying

At Delabole, slate has been quarried for over 600 years, and continuously since the medieval period. Other slate quarries in North Cornwall prospered from the seventeenth century onwards, but now only Delabole continues quarrying at a depth of 500 feet.

Although there have been financial difficulties over the years, slate and stone quarrying continues but modern machinery has replaced the work of hundreds of manual labourers. As a result, local communities have suffered the hardships of mass redundancies similar to those of mining and fishing.

As well as stone quarrying, china clay deposits have been worked extensively on a large scale in Cornwall. Since the 1700s companies have used Cornish china clay in potteries for the production of porcelain and china.

In the environs of St Austell, granite masses originally formed deposits of kaolinite-rich material, which has been extracted by china clay quarrying and commercially exploited. The history of clay mining is a significant part of the social history of the area with whole villages dependent on clay for a livelihood. Many cottages stand today as a memorial to the industry's development over centuries.

In *Black's Guide to Cornwall*, published in 1892, china clay is described to the readers thus:

...it is a species of moist granite – that is, the rock once so firm and

Delabole slate quarry in 1937.

tenacious has been reduced by decomposition into a soft adhesive substance, not unlike mortar, and this, when purified from mica, schorl, or quartz, is admirably adapted for the best kinds of pottery. It is identical with Chines kaolin, or porcelain clay. This is piled in stopes or layers, upon an inclined plane, and a stream of water is then directed over it, which carries with it the finer and purer portions, and deposits them in a large reservoir, while the coarser residuum is caught in pits placed at suitable intervals. From the reservoir all the water is drawn off, and the clay removed to pans, where it is passed under the influence of a novel drying machine, thoroughly relieved of moisture, properly packed up in barrels, and removed to the seaside for shipment.

It was William Cookworthy who bought acres of green fields in Cornwall in 1775 because he recognised it was rich in china clay. Obviously the quarrying process is more complex these days, involving all kinds of mechanised excavation alongside separation and refining technologies that convert kaolinised granite into clay.

In the late-eighteenth century it was Wedgwood, Spode and Minton who sought out the clays quarried in St Austell, but commercial demand increased when clay began to be used in paper-making.

Local merchants began to buy smaller pits until by 1860 approximately

Cornish clay pits at Bugle in 1927.

200 pits were in operation. Specialist suppliers were required to provide the tools, clothing and handmade boots needed for the workers. These associated trades, once local, are now part of a global provision.

Mineral railways were built to serve the quarries and clay areas, transporting between Calstock and Callington and in the nineteenth century, from the china clay districts of Hensbarrow and St Austell. In 1849 the Par and St Blazey to Newquay harbour line was opened. There were specialist china clay shipments from Pentewan and Charlestown, but first the trains in the 1900s, and more recently truck and lorry transport, lost the ports their once-crucial role.

The distinctive kaolin waste tips have shaped the topography of china clay country around St Austell. For every ton of china clay, nine tons of mineral waste is produced creating what appear to be grey/white mountain

The Stannon clay works at St Breward in 1928.

ranges. The unique landscape around the clay district has become a powerful representation of Cornwall's heritage. Conservationists intervene to prevent these artificial hillsides and peaks from being altered or developed. They fight to protect and preserve the landscape and challenge inappropriate plans to expand china clay workings. Conservationists are determined

Charlestown harbour, St Austell, shipping china clay in 1906.

that the physical landscape should not be lost or changed, even if the industrial workings have moved on, leaving the district devoid of its original working purpose.

The company, English China Clays, was formed in the early twentieth century. A French company, Imetal, purchased English China Clays in 1999 to form Imery Minerals Ltd. The future of St Austell's workers remains uncertain, although the company anticipates the continued supply of china clay for numerous products including paint, insecticides and plastics for another decade at least. Despite many hundreds of lost jobs in recent years there continues to be industrial demand for up to half a million tons of clay each year.

Smelting

Smelting would not have been necessary if all tin had come from streaming where weathering had caused the impurities to be washed away and the tin was at its purest.

Smelting involved heating furnaces powered by bellows worked by hand or a water-wheel. The tin, in molten state, would be run off into granite moulds. These original 'blowing-houses' can be dated back to the fourteenth century and were another essential side of the mining industry. Now these derelict buildings are mere remains of a once-fundamental process. Many ruins are scattered across Cornwall, left redundant, their significance barely visible. A water-wheel may indicate a previous smelting place but more often than not

The war memorial and Commercial Road in Hayle, 1926. Hayle was once a centre for smelting and the harbour was a major port for transportation.

wild vegetation has obscured history to the cursory glance of a passer-by.

These smelters were once known as 'white tinners', because they turned the black and brown tin ore, extracted from deep underground mines, into white tin.

At the end of the seventeenth century the industry divided into two distinct sectors: reverberatory furnaces and smelting-houses. Refining and skimming off the dross of molten metal were essential trades once, but have now completely disappeared from Cornwall. From the 1800s smelting hous-es were mainly located in Truro and Penzance, but there were others in Portreath, St Agnes and St Austell.

Hayle was a centre for smelting, but when Harvey & Co. saw that shipments of tin ore were being taken up to Liverpool instead of Hayle they relocated. Today all that remains are the ruined walls, which have been care-fully preserved and converted into a walled playground and recreational area.

Smelting houses along with tin mines, once thriving places of profitable industry, are no more, sometimes leaving behind landscapes of neglect and decay.

Keepers of Light
It was a special kind of person who could cope with weeks of isolation, watching and keeping vigil, stuck out in extremes of weather with just the creatures of the sea for company. The lighthouse keeper is rather a romantic figure, a notion from the past. Today, technological advances mean that lighthouses no longer need a keeper to carry out tasks that were once essential for safeguarding vessels and their crews as they passed dangerous rocks.

The Bishop Rock Lighthouse still stands on the most westerly point of the Isles of Scilly. It was built in 1890 on the most isolated outcrops of the Western Reef and keepers were often stranded there for several weeks at a time. Three successive towers had to be built in this deadly location as the Atlantic sea ravaged and destroyed previous constructions.

One of the most tragic disasters on the Retarrier Rocks close to the Bishop Rock was that of the *Schiller* in 1875. Only 42 souls survived of the 355 on board. A detailed display of the event and its aftermath can be viewed at the island museum on St Mary's.

On 12 December 1992 the last lighthouse keeper left Bishop's Rock. After more than a century of faithful service, a worthy tradition had come to an end. Despite remaining a significant navigational aid, as part of a chain of lights around the Cornish coast including Lizard Point,

The Bishop Rock Lighthouse on the Isles of Scilly in 1911.

Longships and Wolf Rock, Bishop's Rock is surprisingly controlled and monitored from Essex.

The booming blasts of the foghorn, the flashing light, light-float and beacon are now unmanned and are automated by the ingenious use of satellites and other technological devices. The hermit's existence with its

The Lizard lifeboat station, Kilcobben Cove, in 1963 (now disused).

Newquay's lifeboat station was opened in 1861 and these photographs were taken on Lifeboat Day in 1924 (top) and 1928 (bottom).

accompanying tasks of lighting oil-lamps in the lantern room and keeping the fog signal engines maintained is no more. Such sights are consigned to exhibits in museums, while the lighthouses are overseen from computer terminals.

The first lifeboat was built by the townsfolk of Penzance in 1803. This ten-oared, 30-foot-long boat was intended to aid the preservation of life from shipwreck. Cornwall's sea had a terrifying reputation and local residents feared the sorry sights that would be washed ashore so regularly.

It was a slow and steady process but eventually other coastal parishes such as Padstow, Bude, St Agnes, Sennen and St Ives funded their own gallant services and just before 1870 there were fourteen lifeboat stations throughout Cornwall. Most of these stations were closed in the early 1900s and have been replaced by a few select, high-tech launching stations with extraordinary self-righting lifeboats.

Tanneries

Tanners had a crucial and important role in the eighteenth and nineteenth centuries. Most Cornish towns had one or more tanneries close to the meat market, where there would be a ready supply of hides.

Leather has a wide range of commercial and domestic uses. As well as being used for footwear, breeches and outdoor wear, it had agricultural uses too. Saddles, bridles and harnesses, and carriage upholstery all relied on various cuts of leather that had been treated according to its intended future purpose.

The heavy-duty leather came from cattle hides and was tanned during a two-year process. Natural oils were removed and various solutions of oak bark and dog's faeces were applied. Once they were dried out, the curriers would work train oil into the hides until they were pliant. They were then waterproofed with beeswax.

Thinner hides and skins were used for more refined goods such as gloves, sourced from sheep, goats or calves. The process of tanning was much shorter and involved the hanging of hides to remove the fur or wool, followed by a process of beating, soaking and oiling.

Today, in comparison, leather goods are imported from overseas and large-scale tanning is carried out in factories. Leather is now considered to be a fashion accessory rather than an essential product, whereas in the past, the work of a tanner was a much needed and important trade.

Cobblers

Leather goods continue to be made by hand by few specialist craftspeople. Mass production has meant handmade shoes, bags, belts and coats have become items of luxury. Those who can craft bespoke items, made to measure, are now few and far between. PVC riding saddles have substituted the evident need for equestrian leathers and the industrial use of leather goods has been replaced with a wide range of modern synthetic materials. Saddlers tended to work near towns where most of the trade connected to horse-drawn traffic could be taken carried out.

Once shoemaking took place near the hearth at home, or in a small workshop close to the community. The tools needed were basic, and the products were mostly created for functionality rather than fashion. Many villagers and hamlets had shoemakers (cordwainers) and cobblers, who could make and mend shoes. For example, at one time Mousehole had three shoe-makers. They made thigh- and calf-length boots for fishermen before rubber sea boots were available.

Mawnan Smith, as a small rural village in 1841 close to the Helford Passage and four miles from Falmouth with its harbour, was a remote parish with 539 residents inhabiting 127 houses. The parish had 5 shoemakers. A decade later it had 11 in total. It is perhaps important to consider that this was the very time when the Falmouth area was experiencing greater pros-perity, but also several new estates were being built and populated in the Mawnan area. Normally shoes were made to individual requirements, but there were shops in Truro that sold them ready-made. Here in the city there were over 60 cordwainers, many of whom would have had to find alternative employment once mass production of work-wear gained momentum.

Many manual labourers could hardly afford the protective clothing and footwear needed to work in the fields or mines. A farm worker would wear boots with rigid leather, hardened by the wet, without any stockings. A lace hook and shoehorn were essential to get boots on and off as laces would stick fast and be too tough to budge by fingers alone.

Many workers walked tens of miles a day to their employment through all weather conditions. Fields could be sodden and ankle deep in mud or dusty and hot at other times, so it is hardly surprising that the cobbler's service and skill was so much required.

A Working Village

Mawnan Smith, a close-knit community, was indicative of so many Cornish parishes in the early 1800s and as such offers us an example that is repre-sentative of working life in Cornwall at the time of the national censuses conducted in 1811, 1841 and 1851.

Of particular significance are the many livelihoods that sustained a working community and they give us insight into Cornish life in that era. Most notable in the census of 1811 is that 83 per cent of the population of Mawnan were employed in agriculture. All members of the household – men,

Land girls potato planting in Penwith during the Second World War in 1942
precipitated changes in the role of women workers.

women and children – would have worked from as early as 5 a.m. but more usually 6 a.m. By 8 a.m. all the women and children would have been out in the fields, weeding, hoeing, picking up stones, pulling turnips, planting potatoes or scaring birds. Yet these activities were not mentioned in the 1811 or 1841 censuses, unlike the occupations of their husbands. This was at a time when the Women's Suffrage Committee was being formed and numerous unsuccessful bids in Parliament were started for equal rights.

By 1851 married women's work came to be recorded separately; the seamstress's, washerwoman's and charwoman's work by this time being recognised as being exclusive to them and not automatically under their husbands' control. Even so, it was not until 1870 that a woman gained, in certain circumstances, the right to own or control her own earnings. It would not be until more than a century later that her working contribution was lawfully considered to be equal to that of a man's. Only in 1970 did the Equal Pay Act state that a woman should be paid the equivalent of a man who was doing the same work.

Babies were often left at home by necessity, in the care of young girls who carried out household chores in the family's absence. There were all kinds of fatal accidents and serious incidents recorded in Cornwall throughout this period, and although many inquests were brought to the attention of the coroner, stern words were given but no parental prosecutions. Primarily, because parents had no choice, they either left children to fend for themselves, at risk of being burnt, scalded or harmed by animals, or the family starved. In industrial areas the economy relied on child labour as children released the women to work. In larger families older boys and girls were sent into service, either in the estate household or to help daily at one of the local farmhouses.

Gradually, during the early part of the nineteenth century, agriculture lost some of its significance as is indicated in previous chapters. The Mawnan parish reflects a Duchy-wide situation, revealing how new techniques in cultivation

A farrier in St Tudy, 1958. Farriers now travel to the stable and work from a van, whereas in the past all horses were shod in the smithy.

and livestock management on the farms reduced the need for such intensive labour.

A hierarchy of tradesmen and skilled craftsmen were mentioned in the 1841 census. There were ten carpenters, four blacksmiths, five masons,one thatcher, one sawyer, five shoemakers, one bookbinder, one tailor and two dressmakers. Below the small tradesmen and craftsmen came the mass of agricultural labourers and a few other unskilled occupations. There was one road-maker in the village, who was hired by the Vestry.

In most of the main villages and towns there were rope-makers, especially those by the sea. Weavers and mat-makers were known to have exported their wares from West Cornwall, particularly around Sennen.

Mawnan Smith was somewhat fortunate in that new estates were being built in the latter half of the nineteenth century, offering new opportunities for workers of the parish at a time when less labour was needed in agriculture.

There were also a number of blacksmiths. Rough roads meant hard going on shoes for horses as well as men, but Mawnan was also on route to the coast and small inlets were used here for transporting goods by horse-drawn vehicles.

Shops

Nancegollan Post Office in 1938. Nearly all villages had several shops and a post office. Nowadays they struggle to compete with the out-of-town superstores.

Crafthole Post Office in 1909.

In 1841 there was one butcher in Mawnan Smith village, but ten years later four grocers and three pork dealers provided the villagers with food. A mile or so away in the seaside hamlet of Durgan a coal yard supplied fuel that was

Tamar Street, Saltash, in 1906.

Falmouth's Old Curiosity shop in 1905, when each
shop was individual and family-run.

unloaded from boats in the estuary and a coal merchant brought it into the village to the parishioners, who were expected to collect it themselves. There was also an inn and a beer shop in Bareppa, which met the village's needs. Mawnan was well served by three mills in Bosaneth Valley whose product was essential for daily bread. Now we consider a village fortunate if it has a functional post office and/or village store.

By the end of the nineteenth century changes in retailing started to take place as new railways and improved shipping enabled suppliers of goods to keep their prices down. Shops began to trade in new goods such

J. Phillips & Son, Penzance, in 1909.

as stationery, ready-made clothing and pharmaceutical products for the first time.

Truro, because of its unique position close to the coast and international ports, began to offer an expanding range of goods. Silk, lace and cloth from overseas could be acquired together with tobacco, liquor and wines. Sugar, salt, rice, oil, vinegar, pepper, raisins, figs, ginger, soap and candles could all be found in the family-run shops. By this time tea and coffee had started to

161

Terrill & Rodgers Brass and Iron Founders, Redruth, 1906.

be drunk by the professional classes, in preference to beer made from barley malt or the local cider.

But there were also local traders who made their own goods, such as umbrellas, baskets or confectionery in Truro. There were drapers, dress-makers and tailors, hat- and wig-makers, as well as an increasing number of bakers and ironmongers.

In the city it was possible to buy anything from a brass bed to horse clippers, a butter churn to a sewing machine.

Now every town in Britain has its national chain stores, each selling the same range of goods throughout the country. Smaller independent family firms do exist but increasingly the townscape has become predictably uniform and consistent throughout the UK.

Gaze up, however, above the modern graphic of the shop sign, and the original architecture will, for the time being anyway, stand resolutely against conformity. It is obviously far too simplistic to suggest that all towns are now the same but there is some weight to the argument that the multinationals have in some measure robbed our cities of personality.

Thankfully Cornwall's Truro has fought to retain its independent stores. New initiatives are celebrated and supported so that the old-time family-run firm still exists nestled next to the national conglomerate.

Mawnan 1975 Festival sold for 10p

It seems apt that at this stage in the book to include a quote from Mawnan Smith's Festival booklet of 1975. It sums up the sense of impending change but also reflects an awareness that some aspects of life in Cornwall had already been lost by necessity. The writer is unnamed but he or she writes astutely, summing up the dilemma that is still prevalent in Cornish towns and villages – when to embrace change and when to hold on tight to that which remains from the past.

> Until a century ago life in Mawnan Smith, as in every village in the land, showed very little change from one century to the next. Apart from life and death, and a change of parson now and again, things changed very little. Yet, in spite of seeming unchange, life would be lived to the full. There would always be the hard day's work; the gossip and neighbourly interest and kindness in times of need; the joy of loving and being loved; the times of marriage and joy; the sadness of a departing friend. The spring and Autumn of Life would bring together a community strongly knit that loved and cared...

> And now our recent years have wrought great changes. The discovery of new forms of energy, a rapidly growing industrial life, faster means of communication and travel, were bound, in time, to affect every part of our village...

> However much you may want progress to stay in the towns and leave the countryside unchanged, the change is here. Life can never remain as it was, the very word 'life' means growth and change. And Mawnan Smith has changed because Mawnan Smith is alive.

CHAPTER 8

FREE TRADERS

Wrecking is a word that conjures up all manner of stereotypical connotations in the imagination. Murderous rogues dressed in clichéd pirate attire, skulking about on cliff-tops, in coastal caves on foggy nights; caricatures that have been outworked into countless narratives throughout history. These melodramatic figures carried sinister intent, looting cargo from stricken vessels in distress. They were malicious, with scant regard for human life; driven by mercenary motivation they enticed ill-fated ships ashore with their false lights mimicking a safe passage.

Although wrecking was very much a reality in the Cornwall of the past,

The Cornish coast has thousands of hiding places and secret caves from which smugglers may have operated.

the figures described above are thankfully nowadays only found in fiction. The fact that so many incidents of this type of 'looting' took place is perhaps more fairly attributed to the treacherous coastline than a prevalent corrupted nature in the Cornish folk. Wrecking has been taking place all around Britain's coastline since the first ships sailed the oceans.

In reality, wrecking is a term that covers a range of ways to acquire goods from the seashore, from blatant piracy to the mere scavenging of debris cast upon the shore. Flotsam and jetsam, the spoils of a misdemeanour or even tragic incident at sea, have historically meant easy pickings for the sharp-eyed and quick-witted 'beachcomber'. The sea has always been a means of survival for the people of Cornwall; driftwood was used for fires, a supply of staple food could be caught in her waters and any other useful bounty the waves happened to cast up for human use could be salvaged.

For the latter-day Cornish such activity is now generally no more than an occasional hobby, an opportunity to retrieve useful materials, a form of recycling. This is so different from the profitable black-marketeering that took place in the past. Early records confirm the right to wreckage was originally carried out legally by the Crown. Yet as time passed the right to wreck seems to have been vigorously argued by landowners from the 1300s onwards as they laid claim to any salvageable cargo. It was not uncommon for the gentry to be actively involved in retrieving anything of value, in full view of customs officers, if the wreck had taken place in waters directly connected to their own land. Eventually the 'rights' to wreck disappeared and towards the end of the nineteenth century more civilised procedures were implemented.

It is hard to for us to comprehend today how many wrecks actually occurred. There were literally thousands. In earlier centuries local people would have rushed to the scene of a wreck and it is hard to discern whether unfortunate foreigners met with pity or hostility as the plundering of cargo began. Once news of a wreck reached a community, everyone gathered up their tools; pick-axes, crowbars and ropes were carried to the scene to start work on breaking up the vessel. It was considered to be fair plunder once the vessel had touched the shore.

Wrecking was not without dangers of its own and often entire families scrambled on rocks, over high precipices, often in high storms, intent on plundering what they could. This would be hazardous enough in daylight, but work carried on regardless of the hour throughout the night, and many lives were lost in the over-eagerness to carry cargo away.

One example of such a fatal incident took place in St Ives in 1806 when eight men died trying to retrieve a cask of wine or spirits. A ninth man survived to tell the tale by clinging to the oars of the boat.

For anyone who has experienced the thrill of standing close to the shore-line during one of Cornwall's notorious equinoctial storms, when Atlantic waves smash against the rocks in giant white-crested surges, they will no doubt recognise the sensation of dread and awe. These are the times of year when the sea gains ascendancy and reigns supreme, reminding humanity of the formidable force of the water.

Yet if a moment is spent considering the sailing ships of the past, reliant entirely on (often inaccurate) maps, navigational skills and the knowledge of the crew, it is no wonder that upon entering the rocky Cornish waters, espe-cially at night or in fog, so many foundered. Once the sea and wind reached a tumult these vessels were particularly prone to catastrophe, being driven onto the rocks by mighty gale-force winds.

Rescue

Cornwall is flanked by two of Britain's most significant sea-lanes and there-fore had a high density of maritime traffic passing through in the 1800s. If there was a sudden change in weather conditions – a storm starting to brew or fog settling without warning – there were inevitable casualties.

If a night were particularly wild with high winds, the dawn light might reveal more than one vessel broken up upon the shore. It was then that some of Britain's ancient laws and legal stipulations concerning the 'right to wreck', although obsolete, were still perceived as valid by common consensus. The locals' 'public mind' considered the natural law of 'finders keepers' to be of higher precedence than allegiance to the Crown.

Despite Cornwall's reputation for a past of wrecking and smuggling there have always been those individuals who had great compassion for drowning sailors. For centuries there have been self-sacrificing locals who risked their lives in rescuing others from the perils of the sea.

Cornish Hero

It was in December 1807 that Henry Trengrouse saw a hundred men drown from a frigate off the port of Porthleven near Helston. HMS *Anson* was wrecked on Loe Bar, a short distance from Gunwalloe Cove and is one of the most famous wrecks in maritime history. So profound was this tragic experience that Trengrouse devoted the rest of his life to perfecting a system of life-saving apparatus.

Leaving Falmouth just before Christmas Day the lookout ship met a gale and faced difficult seas for several days around Mount's Bay. By the 28th the captain decide to return to Falmouth but mistook Land's End for the Lizard, a mistake that proved to be fatal. It was decided to beach the ship on the sands in order to save lives. For those who have experienced this stretch of coast, they will know it is no exaggeration that waves can cover the tallest of buildings. It was enormous waves such as these that swept the majority on board ship out to sea by the undertow.

Having been born in Mullion in 1772 and brought up on the Lizard, Trengrouse would have been used to shipwreck scenes, yet the enormity of the loss of life that day was shocking in the extreme and he determined to do something about it.

His memorial tombstone in Helston parish church reads:

... ever grateful remembrance of Henry Trengrouse. Of this Borough who, profoundly impressed by the great loss of life by shipwreck, rendered most signal service to humanity, by devoting the greater portion of his life and means, to the invention and adoption of the ROCKET APPARATUS, for communicating between stranded ships and the shore, whereby many thousands of lives have been saved.

They rest from their labours; and their works do follow them.

Others have developed similar inventions and gained more public acclaim, such as John Dennett from the Isle of Wight. However, it is Trengrouse's life-saving rocket device that contributed to saving thousands of lives and was used internationally. Yet he never quite received the kind of recognition or financial reward that he deserved, primarily because he failed to patent his ideas, so that others benefited instead.

Despite suffering financial difficulties in the process and near bankruptcy, he continued in his mission to develop a way of connecting a safety line to distressed vessels offshore. By linking the rescue rope, like a bridge to the ship, passengers could make it safely to land. The initial idea came to him as he watched a firework display. It took a lifetime of personal sacrifice for Trengrouse to perfect his idea to fire a gun or rocket from land as a means of linking this life-line to a wrecked ship.

Completely obsessed and unable to let go of his desire to succeed in his life-saving aim, he put his own personal circumstances in jeopardy. A similar idea was being tested by Captain G. W. Manby, and experiments with mortar throwing a shot earned him a government award.

However, this was too dangerous and cumbersome to be adopted by the authorities. Trengrouse's rocket design was far more efficient and lightweight

Rocket practice in Trevarrian, 1905.

than Manby's yet it took years for Parliament to decide to implement his design. The money Trengrouse received was a small fraction of his outlay and his country failed to give him his due.

Cornwall's North and South Coasts differ considerably in character. The North Coast, with its harsh, bleak ruggedness, has its own catalogue of dire wreck disasters, but it would be wrong to assume that the South Coast had fewer shipwrecks. Despite its wide bays, sheltered estuaries and natural inlets to accommodate passing ships, there are nevertheless headlands projecting unevenly, a cause of grave hazard to shipping. At night-time and in tough weather conditions, it would be difficult to ascertain the precise longitude as the unevenness of the coastline makes it difficult to decipher the exact proximity of jutting rocks. A maritime disaster was more often than not caused by human ignorance, but also by the sheer volume of shipping passing through Cornish waters. Great liners and merchant ships all sailed through the Channel as it was Britain's gateway to the world. Inevitably, with such a bulk of shipping, there would be many accidents and mishaps.

As has been described in previous chapters there were always those willing to risk their lives to assist in rescue missions, and there was never a lack of courage among the fishermen and local communities. A distressed vessel would find a ready response from those waiting to perform a rescue, but there was an interesting dichotomy of intent, as within the same community there were also those waiting to plunder the goods from the foundering vessel. The practice of wrecking and plundering goods reached its peak between 1859 and 1870.

Smuggling

Smuggling has a rich history, being traced back to medieval times when wool was smuggled out from Britain's shores to the continent in order to avoid heavy taxes. Likewise, once the coinage exchanges were introduced into Cornwall for the taxation of tin ore and copper, many early miners found their own ways to avoid the unwelcome costs of officialdom by making use of the isolated coastline and a ready supply of boats. They could make their own way to ships anchored offshore and negotiate better prices with the merchants to avoid paying tax.

Smuggling became widespread in Cornwall and it was almost impossible to prohibit. The Napoleonic Wars meant that navy personnel, normally widely available to represent the Crown and support customs officials, were markedly reduced in number, as they were needed to fight wars in foreign waters. During the French Revolution smuggling experienced a 'golden age' in Cornwall, and nearly every coastal town and village had its contingency working the waters in this way.

The Smugglers' Act of 1736 meant that courts could authorise the death penalty for dangerously wounding customs and excise officers, or for hindering them by force in the execution of their duty. But this didn't seem to prevent the illicit trade. There were lesser penalties for the transportation of goods: up to five years, generally serving in the navy, or doing hard labour for the act of making hand signals within six miles of the coast.

The titled office of Collector of Customs is one of the oldest local government representatives of the Crown. The role entailed giving assistance to vessels in distress, safeguarding the storage of ships and cargoes, and properly supervising shipwreck disasters to protect the interests of merchants and ship owners. They were also charged with the task of detecting smugglers.

The local population heavily outnumbered these official forces and poor communication meant that customs and excise tasks were near impossible. The areas they covered were remote, difficult to access except by foot, dangerously close to precipitous cliffs and with routes requiring local in-depth knowledge to traverse at night. Making such extensive sea patrols in small vessels was both labour-intensive and hazardous in bad weather unless the official crews were well acquainted with the peculiarities of a particular stretch of coastline. The seizing of goods was rare, as an often treacherous approach to the shore safeguarded the rapid movements of the locals. It meant they were often left untroubled by the close attentions of revenue cutters making their sea patrols.

*Mullion Cove, pictured in 2007, was an ideal location in and out of which
smugglers could creep, offload and avoid detection.*

Customs men could do little to stop smuggling despite legislation in 1816
making it far more straightforward for all to comprehend the crime; smuggling was an offence against the Crown, but up until then the law had been
ambiguous in many respects. The practice of disregarding the law in this way
was prevalent and not at all unusual throughout Cornwall. Religious observance and financial integrity in all other aspects of daily life and business was
contradicted by this overt law breaking: a strange combination.

The increasing severity of the law had minimal effect as informers could
rarely be found in isolated coastal regions. Witnesses 'noticed nothing' despite
huge rewards being offered by the authorities, the truth being, that loyalty within village communities ran deep because the entire village relied on smuggling
for survival. People knew they needed to turn a blind eye and ignore 'mysterious goings on'. To wake at night and hear the sound of packhorses or other
'strange doings' was something to cast from one's mind and conscience. For the
majority of Cornish folk, honest and law abiding in all other respects, smuggling
or 'free trading' was perceived to be outside the remit of law.

The further establishment of customs and excise law meant that experienced smugglers needed to employ more subtlety and cunning because more

THE CORNISH MAGAZINE

An illustration from the first Cornish Magazine *of a smuggling boat with tubs of brandy or rum slung ready for sinking. Sinking stones are kept on deck until just before slipping into the water.*

overt methods of old were no longer feasible. Customs watchmen were potentially posted at every creek and headland making it extremely risky to land during daylight hours. New methods became commonplace – sinking cargoes then afterwards 'working' and picking up the goods as and when opportunity arose.

Even if customs and excise officials were successful in seizing looted cargo, they would invariably be set upon, bound and gagged, and taken to be dumped alive elsewhere out of 'harms way' until a job was completed.

Typically, when a wreck took place, some of the community would be involved in the rescue operation while others secured the cargo to smuggle it ashore. Lookouts would be posted to wait for the official delegation to arrive, although more often than not they failed to turn up if an informer had not

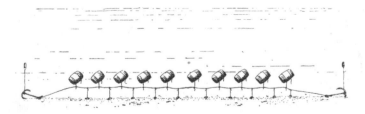

A crop of goods after sinking, waiting to be 'worked', when the smugglers could be sure that their movements in the water would not arouse suspicion.

The Ship Inn at Porthleven, built 300 years ago, is reported to have been a favoured smugglers' haunt with an easy lookout to the bay.

made it to the coastguard in time, the lookouts sounding the alarm as the customs approached. Even if the customs' men were armed, many smugglers matched their strength and were known to violently set upon opponents with cudgels if they stood in the way of their business interests. The law had little hold on such a hardy and scattered population.

The whole community was in cahoots as they pursued ingenious methods of securing portions of the smugglers' contraband. Many cottages along the coast still have secret cavities for holding goods in cellars and passageways. There are tales of brandy being stored in lobster pots, tobacco in special hidey-holes up chimneys, hollow books made for storing tea, and fishermen stuffing lace down their boots. Women faked pregnancies and unbelievably waddled up the quay with a keg up their skirt, or with an extra heavy basket of laundry. Water barrels were specially made with separate secret compartments to transport spirits inside. Boats had false keels to artfully conceal all the luxury goods on a voyage. There were many tricks of the trade and women took a very active part in the artistry of secreting goods and disposing of contraband.

Gunwalloe Church, north of Mullion Cove has a tunnel that led under

Gunwalloe Church in 2007. Isolated and cut off from main thoroughfares,
it is easy to see why this made such an ideal location for smuggling.

the cliffs and was used to unload goods from smaller vessels. It emerges next
to the church. There are countless tales of tombs and coffins being used to
stow away goods by daring free traders in the shadowy light of dawn.

Locals had obvious immediate advantages on the frontline, becoming
organised large-scale business operations by the late 1800s. They knew the
coastline intimately and worked together as a closely affiliated team. Once a
large smuggling vessel was spotted on the shore the crews of smaller craft
made their way to offload, operating swiftly. The goods could either be
brought ashore or stored on cliffs or in caves to be retrieved later by climb-
ing down rope ladders if the tide was in.

Penzance, Mousehole, Mullion, St Ives, Porthgwarra, Hayle, Porthcothan,
Polperro, Cawsand Bay, St Mawes, Gweek and Mylor were all famous for their
long histories of smuggling. These locations struggled with unemployment
from deep economic recessions in fishing and agriculture so free trading was a
means of providing for families in hard times. Such tight communities, with so
many unemployed, were able to hold fertile discussions and organise extensive
operations, their boldness and ingenuity outwitting any official investigations.
Free traders had a whole community of willing accomplices at their disposal

The estuary reaches the river bridge at Gweek (2007), a place renowned for clandestine smuggling activities.

whose otherwise extreme poverty was greatly alleviated by the profits from smuggling.

When the long wars with France came to an end at the beginning of the nineteenth century and the fighting services of the Crown were reduced, a large number of navy servicemen became privateers and as such could easily smuggle 'on the side'. Professionals of all kinds were involved, even magistrates and religious leaders who knew that it was only illegal to bring smuggled goods ashore but not to consume or trade in them.

As Rudyard Kipling's popular poem, 'A Smuggler's Song', illustrates, it was advisable for all to 'look to a wall', meaning to look elsewhere, when the smugglers brought their illegal goods of tea, brandy, tobacco, lace or silk ashore and through the streets in daylight hours. The less seen meant less to confess later under oath and mothers would train their children to turn their backs to the 'gentlemen riding by'.

Smuggler's Tales
John Carter is one such gentleman and probably the most infamous of Cornish smugglers, who went under the pseudonym of 'the King of Prussia'.

Prussia Cove in 2007, east of Cudden Point, where a little harbouring point is cut out of the solid cliff bedrock. Packhorses and 'barrel men' carrying barrels of spirits to Carter's residence nearby served this remote area.

The oft-told story goes that he named himself this in a childhood game of soldiers and the nickname stuck: so much so that the cove out of which he operated his notorious smuggling enterprise changed over time from Porthlea or King's Cove to Prussia Cove. Prussia Cove today is unspoilt and remains secluded, away from the main tourist spots. In Carter's day the only way of accessing the cove was by bridle path.

The Carters were a respected and upright family of eight brothers, who were all involved in smuggling spirits from France between 1777 and 1807. John's trading in luxury goods was respected by all. He was known to be a man of his word and could be trusted to supply goods efficiently. It was because of his honest reputation that he became so distressed when the customs and excise men raided his home while he was away and seized a quantity of brandy, taking it to the custom house in Penzance.

Carter was apparently so troubled on his return home, not for being raided but for letting his customers down. He valued his trustworthy reputation and so retaliated by breaking into the custom house with the help of a body of men known as the 'Cove Boys'. He had given his word that he would

A storage shed above Prussia Cove in 2007.

deliver the consignment, so he determined to keep his promise. Because he only retrieved his own barrels of spirits it was obvious he was responsible and the customs men recognised that no one else would have been as honest as the King of Prussia.

John's brother, Captain Harry Carter, converted to Methodism and recorded parts of his smuggling life, although he gave up the practice after Wesley's teaching. It was Harry who spent most of his time at sea while John managed things on shore and lived near the cove. John managed the actual landing and disposal of the cargoes that Harry brought into the cove from places such as Roscoff in Brittany.

It is still possible to see the landing area in the cove that was carved out of the granite rock to make Harry's delivery of provisions such as beef and bread easier to offload. Once they were brought up the steep cliff path on foot they were stored in John's locked shed.

Customs officers paid a visit to the cove one day and found John's shed locked and demanded to inspect its contents. The King of Prussia refused saying there was nothing more inside than provisions for his brother's vessel. The officers proceeded to break the door down despite John's protestations. John made it clear and warned them that he would require recompense should any of his possessions be put in jeopardy and vulnerable to thieves by the officers breaking off the lock and door. The officers' venture inside the shed was in vain as Carter was true to his word and the shed was indeed full of hidden reserves for his brother's ship. Frustrated the officers retreated but with Carter repeating that he would call on them again should any of his provisions get lost or damaged. Indeed it transpired as he predicted; as he slept his shed was cleared of valuable equipment and sure enough the unfortunate officers of the Crown compensated him.

The most famous incident involving conflict with the Crown from Prussia Cove involved firing at a revenue cutter. The Battery Rocks, situated at a point between Bessie's Cove and King's Cove, made an ideal escape point for a smuggler in his small boat one time as he was being pursued by a revenue cutter. The smuggler took his boat along a narrow rocky channel that the cutter did not dare to negotiate. John Cornish, writing in the *Cornish Magazine* of 1899, read and quoted the Custom's log book of 1769. He finishes the tale:

> The King, with his merry men, opened fire on the boat. They loaded up the little guns so that every time they fired the guns kicked over completely backwards, and had to be replaced. The boat was driven back, and the cutter held off for the night. Next morning the fight was renewed, the cutter opening fire from the sea, while a company of 'riders' fired from the hedge at the top of the hill on the rear of the men in the battery. This turned the tables on the smugglers, who sought shelter in Bessie Bussow's house. The boys, of whom Will Richards was one (he died about 1855, aged eighty-five), were out behind the house; and as the cutter's shot struck in the soft cliff, they ran with a 'tubbal' and dug them out. All this time Uncle Will Leggo was ploughing in the little garden just above the house, and his old sister Nan was leading the horses. Someone went to him and suggested that it was dangerous, and he had better 'leave out'.
>
> 'Now, theer,' said Uncle Will, 'I've bin thinkan of Nan and the 'osses this bra while,' which shows a fine contempt either for the serious intentions or for the marksmanship of H. M. seamen and the riders. The firing produced little effect, or was apparently not followed up in any way, for there the story somewhat abruptly ends.

In those days smuggling was carried out on large cutters or luggers, which were armed with up to 20 guns each but in later years 27-foot gigs were used and small open sailing boats proved more convenient.

Another ingenious way of avoiding the seizure of booty took place in Prussia Cove so the story goes, this being a smuggler's version. Two of Carter's men were rowing home from Roscoff, and as they pulled into Mullion they found two customs officers waiting for their return. They attempted to bribe them, as was often the practice, but the officers were not persuaded from their course of action. So the men rowed on around the coast with the officers pursuing them along the cliffs on horseback. For a while the officers lost sight of the men as they approached the headland, as it was here that the smugglers were able to negotiate a change of boats with a local fisherman who was hauling crab pots. The men finally rowed into Prussia Cove and when the officers arrived they searched the boat to no avail. Some time later, when the coast was clear and all the fuss had died down, a seemingly innocent crabber brought his catch ashore and two 'kindly fellows' cheerfully helped to carry his crab pots.

At this time it was a serious offence to make a light to signal off the coast and there was a hefty fine or a penalty of at least twelve months' hard labour. Captain Will Richards, who lived at Bessie's Cove, worked and lived with old Hoskins and his apprentice, who went under the guise of being ship's carpenters. These two accomplices were rowing home from France and were expected to be back about nine at night. However, Richards received a tip off that the custom house boat was lurking just off Cudden for most of the day.

Ever resourceful, and aware of the risks that awaited Hoskins and the young man if they were captured, he endeavoured to warn them. Taking an armful of 'after-winding' (chaff from the threshing floor) he set it alight up his chimney so that the blaze roared out of the top to warn the men of danger. It was apparently visible from miles out to sea so one can only imagine the risks that 'Cappen' Will made, nearly burning down his house. The cargo was safely landed and stored temporarily in an old shaft.

Next day, packhorses, as planned, were ready and waiting to transport the goods from Trenowl's farm at the top of the hill when four custom house men arrived.

All the smugglers assumed an air of idleness and nonchalance and all was quiet in Bessie's Cove for the entire afternoon. As the weather took a turn and a squall arose as night drew in, ever hospitable Cappen Will showed much concern for the officers when he realised they had left without food or drink. He had Mrs Richards make the men some broth and invited them in out of the cold but advised them not to come in all at once in case another officer came along and found them inside.

'Oh, no officer won't come along tonight,' they assured him, a slip of the tongue that gave Richards the reassurance he needed to carry on with his plan. The Cappen pressed on them that he thought it safer if they did as he advised under the pretence that he did not want the watchmen to get into trouble. After a bowl of broth and a 'gaddle' of warm grog they were satisfied and went to relieve the other two watchmen. They, too, were treated to Mrs Richard's cooking. By this time the wind and rain had come in strong, so Cappen Will took some warm grog to the men outside in the dark.

Meanwhile, taking their time to savour the warm fire and rest awhile the men indoors became comfortable much to the annoyance of the two out of doors. Twice the watchmen knocked on the door only to find that the meal was still in progress and their associates were contentedly enjoying the food and warmth. Unable to resist the lure of the fire anymore, all the men gave up on the watch and yielded to the Cappen's hospitality at last. Long before those men made their way home in the early hours, the hidden kegs were out of the shaft, carried by tub men (men carrying barrels strapped over their shoulders) or loaded on packhorses and gone.

A customs collector in Penzance wrote to his superior in London on 29 June 1775 where he refers to the 'great audacity of the smugglers on this coast', he continues:

Last Saturday two Irish wherries full of men and guns (one about 130 tons, and the other less) came to anchor within the limits of this port, and within half a mile of the shore, and lay there three days, in open defiance discharging their contraband goods. We are totally destitute of any force to attack them by sea, and, as the whole coast is principally inhabited by a lot of smugglers under the denomination of fishermen, it is next to an impossibility for the officers of the revenue to intercept any of these goods after they are landed, unless by chance a trifling matter. The smugglers escort their goods in large parties when on shore. A few nights ago, while the above-mentioned wherries were on the coast, the officers, being on the look-out, saw a boat come off from one of them and come ashore near where the officers had secreted themselves, and the crew began to land the goods. The officers interfered, and attempted to make a seizure of said boat and goods; but a blunderbuss was immediately presented to one of their breasts, and the smugglers, with great imprecations, threatened their lives. The officers, not being of sufficient force, were glad to get off, and the boat reshipped the goods and went off again. We humbly beg leave to remark the smugglers were never on this coast more rife than at present, nor less goods taken in proportion to the quantity supposed to be smuggled.

A similar outright defiance to the law took place on 29 November 1777 when an Irish wherry armed and manned towed away the *Brilliant* with the captain on board. The *Brilliant*, a shallop used by the revenue, was full of captured cargo, but the free traders took all their goods back off her and turned the *Brilliant* adrift at sea.

It seems that the request for soldiers to support customs was constantly being reiterated to the Crown's services in London and from time to time additional assistance was provided. However, it was sporadic and, while it lasted, effective, but once the soldiers were posted elsewhere the situation returned to normal. In 1769 the customs collector writes:

> ... the soldiers now quartered in this town are most useful. They are a great terror to the smugglers. The mayor of Penzance has always paid for fire and candles for the guardroom, but the present mayor refused to do so. At this I do not wonder, as he is at present bound over in a large sum not to be again guilty of smuggling.

Cawsand Bay

> *In Cawsand Bay lying, with the Blue Peter flying,*
> *and all hands on deck for the anchor to weigh,*
> *We spied a young lady, as fresh as a daisy,*
> *And modestly hailing, this damsel did say –*
>
> *Ship ahoy! Bear a hand there! I wants a young man there,*
> *So heave us a man-rope, or send him to me:*
> *His name's Henry Grady, and I am a lady*
> *Arrived to prevent him from going to sea.*

Cawsand Bay was not only the place where the navy fleets gathered but also the headquarters for smuggling in the West. Because of its close proximity to Plymouth it was straightforward to dispose of cheap spirits, French brandy and tobacco in such a thriving population centre. It must have taken an immense amount of enterprise and daring ingenuity to carry out trafficking of illicit goods in such close proximity to the naval officers.

Smuggling Days and Smuggling Ways was written in 1892 by Commander the Hon. Henry N. Shore (later known as Lord Teignmouth). He was an inspecting officer of HM Coastguard in the late-nineteenth century and gathered material for his book from official sources as well as collecting personal anecdotes.

In the *Cornish Magazine*, at the turn of the twentieth century, on the Cawsand men in 'Annals of the Smugglers' he wrote:

> For a couple of centuries Cawsand was so closely bound up with the navy, that for the navy it may be said to have lived and moved and had its being; and assuredly such prosperity as the place ever attained to was chiefly due to its connection with the naval service.

He documents how the termination of the French war enabled the Crown to focus naval resources towards the activities of smugglers as never before. It is interesting that the end of fighting overseas also precipitated a surge in ex-naval officers using their seamanship knowledge and skill by turning to smuggling as privateers.

The Crown was able to support a new preventative service for the first time in history, using the large number of readily available soldiers and sailors. There were financial rewards offered as incentive for officers to use their talents and expertise in capturing smugglers rather than becoming free traders themselves.

It would be easy to assume that, with such a body of able officers in the vicinity, smugglers would not have the brazenness and daring to carry out their activities under such close scrutiny. But this was not the case. A great many successful enterprises were carried out by Cawsand men, not only in their own neighbourhood but also working in the waters along the North Channel all the way to Padstow. Shore writes:

> At what period of the world's history the men of Cawsand took to illicit trading cannot be now affirmed with any certainty; but to them when the final history of Cornish smuggling comes to be written, the place of honour will probably be awarded. Nor has the haven long ceased to cherish the persons still living, when old cronies, gossiping with the stranger, would speak regretfully of the 'good old days' when money was 'that plentiful' in Cawsand that if one woman went to borrow of another the friend in need would measure out guineas by the basinful.

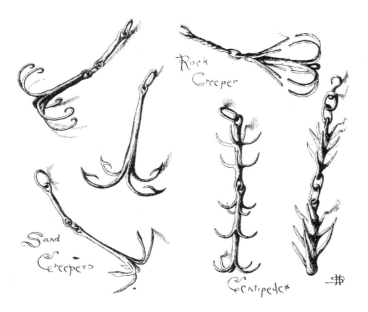

Implements used by coastguards to capture goods in the sea.

He goes on to write about the wealth that Cawsand enjoyed:

> 'When I was stationed at Cawsand, long ago,' said a very old Coast
> guard pensioner to the writer, 'I well remember a poor old fellow
> named P_____, almost bent double with age, who often came
> down to the beach to hunt about for spade guineas. You see, guineas
> were so plentiful in old time that I've heard it said chaps used to
> play pitch-and-toss with them, just as the youngsters do now with
> ha'pence.'
>
> Whence arose this tradition? Possibly the reckless way in
> which the smugglers in the halcyon days of the 'trade' were wont to
> squander their ill-gotten gains – for the profits of a successful trip
> were often enormous – may have given rise to an exaggerated
> notion of the wealth of the community. And I am the more inclined
> to accept this as the true explanation, seeing that precisely the same
> story has been told to me in other Cornish havens.

Whitsand Bay was a particularly favourable spot for sinking cargo and
Shore drew his own illustrations of implements devised to seize kegs from
under water.

The lengths to which smugglers resorted were extraordinary. Specialist boats were built but others were also adapted for smuggling purposes, as Shore explains:

> But what chiefly enabled the Cawsand men to take the lead was their possession of a class of boat which exactly suited the requirements of the trade. The large craft, cutters, and luggers of a hundred tons and more – half smugglers and half privateers – which had been employed during the war, and carried guns, not always for fighting the French, were no longer available. An armed smuggler was a pirate, pure and simple, and could never be tolerated in peace time. Moreover; most of these vessels, even if not worn out and consigned to the ship-knacker's yard, were far too large for bona-fide smuggling. A much smaller class of vessel was now required, as being less liable to detection and handier in every way for the 'running' of illicit goods on a guarded coast.
>
> It so happened that Cawsand Bay fishing boats exactly met these requirements, and being half-decked, excellent sea boats, and of remarkably good sailing qualities, they came into immediate request.

The high profits made in the trading of contraband was an incentive for smugglers to take great risks in crossing the English Channel in small open boats. Obviously only a few tubs could be brought back in such flimsy craft and one can hardly imagine the hazardous miles of stormy sea that these men were prepared to cross, risking their all. The more ambitious traders, who aimed at cargoes of a hundred tubs or more, required for the safe conveyance of their wares a larger class of boat than was to be met with at that time in fishing villages along the Cornish coast.

A full range of vessels was built in Cawsand, the most popular being outwardly for working the seine nets, but adapted and purpose-built for smuggling. Because of their light framework the six- and eight-oared craft could move at great speed. All kinds of suitable smuggling vessels could be built to particular specifications at Cawsand.

This port more than any other was equipped to conduct free trade, but the risks of being seized by the authorities were higher than anywhere else. All manner of pseudo runs were set up to hoax the customs officers, and complex plans were devised to send the revenue cutters in the wrong direction. Tip-offs would be fabricated, smugglers would set off under pretence, carefully shadowed by the officers only to have the genuine smugglers outwit them by going elsewhere. All sorts of trickery and intrigue were devised.

Because a series of specialist boats had been plundered and destroyed, after they were found to be used for contraband, smugglers began to employ French boats instead of risking using their own vessels. By chartering French vessels the revenue cruisers could not interfere with them once they were outside territorial waters. So by bringing goods over the sea in freights they could then sink them in convenient spots.

Even though the landing of contraband became ever more complex, the efficiency to which the entire network of helpers operated was astounding. Once the cargo was brought ashore, it was laid up in innumerable caves, barns, wells, hayricks and other hiding places. The success of these clandestine missions relied entirely on the trust between all concerned and it could well be that the Cornish motto 'One and All' came from such tight bonds of loyalty.

The end of the smuggling trade was not sudden or absolute. It went into decline over a period of years and as late as the 1870s smuggling still continued in some of the more isolated ports. The Coastguard Act of 1856 gave control of the coast to the Admiralty, which in many respects made smuggling life more difficult and complicated than ever before. It was no longer so economically viable, and the risk of capture was so much greater.

Daniel and William

One notorious passenger ship, noted in official records time and time again, and under constant suspicion for smuggling, was the *Daniel and William* of Portsmouth. She was known to be employed in the conveyance of goods and passengers between Portsmouth and Plymouth in the 1830s. However, it was reported that she was also known to be in the habit of visiting France for contraband, and in 1832 it was noted in the preventivemen's records that she had been to Roscoff on a smuggling trip.

She gained the infamous reputation of being one of the most successful smuggling crafts in that era, and despite being constantly monitored, she managed to evade capture.

She made frequent trips to Cornwall, particularly Downderry, a village in Whitsand Bay that was the former home of two of her crew. The preventivemen had a strong belief that she was sinking her cargo off Downderry.

Suspicions concerning this vessel grew as she was reported leaving Plymouth waters with a well-known Millbrook smuggler on board.

An informant from Roscoff kept the British customs authorities well informed and was able to divulge how on one occasion a consignment of contraband had been stowed away and concealed underneath her hull. She had apparently made several successful smuggling trips by hiding her cargo in such an inventive way.

She was known to have made several trips to Looe, although she was also known to aim for Fowey district if there was any sense of being chased by the admiral's tender.

Once the authorities came aboard they always looked for certain signs, such as sinking-stones, French bread, or the smell of spirits. If a vessel had a small number of men on board and was perhaps missing a small boat there was an indication that cargo had recently been landed.

Even though officials may have had strong suspicions, it was absolutely essential for them to find contraband on board before they could condemn a vessel. Although the *Daniel and William* made many spurious voyages to Penzance, to Cawsand and back to Roscoff, officials failed to find absolute evidence. Eventually, however, she was caught and condemned for smuggling, brought into Fowey harbour and systematically sawn in three as a penalty.

In many ways the *Daniel and William* represented the audacity of the

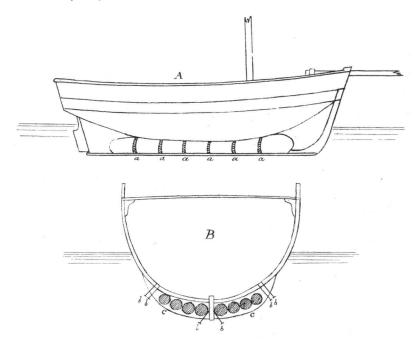

The illustration from the Cornish Magazine *by Shore explains how the* Daniel and William *became so successful for such a long time.*

Cornish smugglers but also demonstrates how ingenious they could be in order to survive. Admittedly, it is debatable whether we should admire this form of ingenuity in conspiring against the law, but there can be some appreciation of the daring needed to succeed against all odds. It is this same daring that enabled the Cornish to mine deep underground, and to sail or fish along the brutal coastline.

By the late 1840s the heights of Cornish smuggling were over and free trading was carried on in a less extensive way. Some have cited Methodism as the main reason for communities turning against the practice, while others consider it to have been because the HM Customs became more organised and effective.

Smuggling will always continue but now the majority of people considers such activities as drug and immigrant trafficking to be highly dubious and would most likely distance themselves from being involved in any way.

Long gone are the days when the entire community worked together, each with a part to play in the complex process of free trading. Such organised activity, with so many acting as outlaws, was a phenomenon of a specific time and it is hard to imagine so much widespread criminal behaviour being considered by the majority as perfectly acceptable, honourable even, or a valid dissenting cause.

No more will tinner, farmer, squire and lady all work together, united in their quest for illicit gain with a common enemy, the excise men. There was an honourable code of conduct among all the fair traders, a sense of deep loyalty no one dared to breech by betrayal. Such strong affiliations throughout an entire community are hard to envisage nowadays.

BIBLIOGRAPHY

Addicoat, I. & Buswell, G., *Mysteries of the Cornish Coast*, Halsgrove
    Discover Series, 2003.

Antony, D., *A Book About Smuggling in the West Country 1700–1850*,
    Hippisley Coxe, Tab House, Padstow, 1984.

Barnicoat, D., *Dodman to Black Head: A Pictorial Study of the Tall Ships and
    Falmouth in the Days of Sail*, Packet Publishing, Cornwall, 1998.

Barton, R.M. and Bradford, D. (eds), *Life In Cornwall In The Mid Nineteenth
    Century*, Barton Ltd, Truro, 1971.

Besley, H., *Handbook of Western Cornwall*, 1852.

Blacks, *Guide to Cornwall, 1892*, Adam & Charles Black, London, 1892.

Bowden, T., *Britain in Old Photographs*, Cornwall, Sutton Publishing,
    Phoenix Mill, 2005.

Buckley, J., *The Cornish Mining Industry*, Tor Mark, 2002.

Cook, Judith, Hardie, Melissa and Payne, Christina, *Singing From the Walls:
    The Life and Art of Elizabeth Forbes*, Sampson and Company in
    association with Penlee House Gallery and Museum, 2000.

The Cornish Magazine, Truro, 1899.

Corin, J., *Fishermen's Conflict*, Tosp'l Books, 1988.

Corin, J., *Sennen Cove and its Lifeboat*, The Sennen Cove Branch of the
    Royal National Lifeboat Institution, Penzance, 1985.

Earl, B., *Cornish Mining: The Techniques of Metal Mining in the West of
    England, Past and Present*, Cornish Hillside Publications,
    St Austell, 1994.

Graham F., *Smuggling in Cornwall*, Clarke Publications, Dorset (no date).

Henwood, G., *Cornwall's Mines and Miners*, Bradford Barton Ltd,
    Truro, 1972.

Jenkin, A.K. Hamilton, *The Cornish Miner*, David & Charles Reprints,
    Newton Abbot, Devon, 1927.

Kittridge, A., *Cornwall's Maritime Heritage*, Twelveheads Press, 2003.

Lanely, M. and Small, Edwina, *Lost Ships of the West Country*, Stanford Maritime, London, 1988.

Leach, N., *Cornwall's Lifeboat Heritage*, Twelveheads Press (no date).

Lean, T., *Steam Engines in Cornwall*, Bradford Barton Ltd, Truro, 1969.

The Netherton and Worth Tourists' Guide to Cornwall, 1900.

Martin, C., *Cornish Inventors*, Tor Mark Press, 2001.

Morris, J. (ed.) *The Domesday Book (Cornwall)*, Phillimore, Chichester, 1979.

Noall, C. and Farr, G., *Rescue Round the Cornish Coast*, D. Bradford Barton Ltd, Truro, 1971.

Noall, C., *Botallack: Monographs on Mining History*, D. Bradford Barton Ltd, Truro, 1972.

Noall, C., *Geevor: Geevor Tin Mines*, 1983.

Orme, N., *Unity and Variety: A History of the Church in Devon and Cornwall*, University of Exeter Press, Exeter, 1991.

Payton, P., *Cornwall Since the War*, Institute of Cornish Studies, 1993.

Payton, P., *Cornwall's History: An Introduction*, Tor Mark, 2002.

Pitts, E.J., *Mawnan 1975 Festival Booklet, The People and their Occupations*, (The Parish of Mawnan) 1760–1860.

Shaw, T., *A History of Cornish Methodism*, Oscar Blackford Ltd, 1967.

Stanier, P., *Cornwall's Mining Heritage*, Twelveheads Press, Truro, 1988.

Smelt, A., *101 Cornish Lives*, Alison Hodge, Penzance, 2006.

Todd, A.C. and Laws, Peter, *Industrial Archeology of Cornwall*, Latimer Trend and Company Ltd, Plymouth, 1972.

Western Morning News, *Cornwall Since 1900: 100 Years of Photographs*, Plymouth, 1990.

Whetter, J., *Cornwall from the Newspapers 1781–93*, The Roseland Institute, Goran, 2000.

INDEX